Searching For T
A School's Jo
Recovery

By

Christan Upton

ISBN: 9798762231183

The author does not wish to profit from the sale of this book therefore any profits will be donated to charity.

To an amazing little girl whom we all miss every day, her incredible friends, and a dedicated and loving team of professionals.

About the Author

Chris Upton is an experienced head teacher and teacher, having led two very different primary schools in the county of Lancashire in North West England. He has also worked as an executive head teacher for a short spell, leading a Pupil Referral Unit. He has a wide range of experience in education in differing roles, and is someone who has always found innovative ways to support young people throughout. These include setting up a brass band in a deprived area and working collaboratively to improve swimming services for disadvantaged pupils, as well as taking an active role in the strategic development of school sport that has a focus on physical activity, not just on competitive sport. More recently, Chris worked as a group of five schools to set up the Axia Learning Alliance, Lancashire's first Mutual Co-operative Foundation Trust.

Originally from the island of Jersey, Chris has a keen interest in music and sport, although he spends most of his time in his personal life with his wife, Lucy, and his four children.

Preface

We have all watched terrible incidents occur on the news, having that human urge to find out more to satisfy our insatiable thirst for information. That is, until a new story comes along. But what if your life becomes intertwined with a story? You have people looking at you for direction and, no matter how low you feel, you have no option but to do the right thing and keep going.

Searching for the Sparkle is a book that reflects on the real-life events that affected Tarleton Community Primary School in the aftermath of the terror attack at the Manchester Arena on 22 May 2017. Sadly, the youngest of the twenty-two victims, at only eight years of age, was a much-loved member of the school. Her name was Saffie-Rose Roussos and her picture and story is known around the world.

This book reflects this story and the work of leading a school through recovery in an unprecedented situation for a UK primary school to face, and is written from my perspective as the head teacher of the school. It aims to provide an insight into what it is like to lead a school family, responding to their needs throughout such a challenging and traumatic period: the many downs, but also the ups. The best and worst of humanity, as well as the strength of a staff team who have focused on supporting the mental health and well-being of their pupils past and present so that they are able to thrive, despite the unjust terror and fear that has gatecrashed their childhoods. In short, searching for that little sparkle so that they could be children again.

The twists and turns that have occurred in the years following the attack may surprise you. When I have spoken about them professionally, it always seems to shock the audience, but also leads them deep into their own thoughts about how they might deal with the various issues that have arisen. Ultimately, professionals from a variety of areas (including education) will have had a range of counterterrorism training, reflecting on preventing attacks and identifying potential threats to the authorities appropriately. However, there seems to be little training and experience that reflects on what happens after an attack, what to expect, and, most importantly, how to support people of varying ages in their journey of recovery.

This book provides a unique perspective on the highs and lows of recovery, using firsthand experiences, with the aim of informing and supporting others. If the effects of terrorism could reach Tarleton Community Primary School, then they could reach any of you. The work that has occurred behind the scenes has always focused on learning from such a unique situation and ensuring that, should another school go through a similar situation, they are well supported.

It must also be remembered that, despite what the community has gone through, no one can imagine the continued pain and suffering of the Roussos family, who wake up every day without their beloved little girl. Theirs is a life sentence.

Throughout the recovery process, I have always maintained contact with Andrew and Lisa Roussos, Saffie's parents. This has been important at key times in the recovery process, such as the first anniversary of their daughter's death. We have always spoken openly as the excruciating issues have arisen, and the family have always been fully aware that this book was being written – without their blessing, you simply wouldn't be reading it now.

Many people over the last few years have told me to write this book. Not only to highlight the need for continued support for the victims of terror, but also because it is an unbelievable true story of doing the right thing, battling for support, and the kindness of both strangers and celebrities, with a beautiful little girl at its centre who must never be forgotten.

Introduction

How do you tell two hundred and seventy-six primary school-aged children that their friend has died? Even worse, that they have died in the most terrible circumstances? Murdered in a terror attack. There is no answer to that question, and it is a question that few people would ever consider, let alone need to answer. It was certainly a question that I had never considered, and yet the day before I was forced to do so, I stood blissfully unaware, welcoming children and their parents into our school as I always did. Their world and mine, like so many others, would soon change forever.

I was eight months into my second headship in the Lancashire village of Tarleton, approximately ten miles south west of the city of Preston and, after the initial battles you face when taking over a school, things were going well. Having upset the locals by stopping the afternoon drop-offs in the school car park, I'd been forgiven, and the staff were getting used to my impatience.

On that particular morning, 22 May 2017, I was greeted by some very excited sisters who came to hurriedly tell me that they were going to a concert that evening at the Manchester Arena. 'Who are you going to see?' I asked. The simultaneous and enthusiastic reply came straight back at me: 'Ariana Grande'. I didn't hide the fact that I had never heard of her. I was a man in my late thirties, much above my fighting weight, and certainly did not fit the demographic of her fan base. I teased them, asking if they wanted to listen to some proper music instead, perhaps some Iron Maiden – a band, of course, that they had never heard of. I guess that is the great thing about music; different artists affect us all differently. I was delighted for them, though. What lucky girls, to go to such a concert at such an iconic venue – they were surely the envy of their friends, and I looked forward to seeing them bounce into school the next day to tell me all about it. This, of course, would never happen.

The rest of the day was much like any other. The general routines of running a primary school: dropping into classes, picking up emails, meetings and the odd bit of paperwork, and

1

then back out on the gate at the end of the school day – something I have always done to ensure that, as a head teacher, parents and children have access to me, so that any niggly issues can be resolved and the children leave happy.

Like most people, I went to bed that evening without a care in the world. I was fast asleep when the incidents in Manchester began to unfold.

Chapter One

We have all woken up with that feeling that something is wrong. A hazy uncertainty that makes you sleepily reach out, fumbling around the top of your bedside drawers, searching for your phone. The 23 May 2017 was one of those mornings for me. As I opened my phone, the inevitable BBC News notification was on, as well as other notifications for varying social media apps. As I began flicking through them, my heart sank. There had been a terror attack at the Manchester Arena. This was a mere twenty-two miles from where I was living. How could this have happened? How bad was it? Then something dawned on me – my conversation on the gate yesterday. I felt sick. Quickly, I dashed to the shower, as I needed to get to school to phone the family of the children I'd spoken with, to make sure they were OK. The journey to school felt like the longest and most irritating drive of my life, as I hit every red light and got stuck behind every tractor and lorry in the county. I was pleased to pull up at school, the signage of Tarleton Community Primary School catching the reflection of the warm morning sun from their position on two tall red brick chimneys.

Rushing into my office, I fired up the computer, which seemed to take an age – such is the joy of working in a rural village when it comes to internet speed. I made the call, holding my breath until the mother of the sisters answered the phone. Physically, they were OK. I cannot describe my feeling of relief at this news, although it broke my heart, as the conversation unfolded, to hear of the incident at what was essentially a concert for children and young people. The horrors that the young audience had witnessed: the confusion, the fear. Why? How could anyone target the innocent in such a way? We would do everything to support the girls and their family to get through this, but it was such an early point for them to process what had happened. We agreed to keep things as normal as possible for them and provide any support that would be needed in the coming days and months ahead. The call ended and I sat at my desk, deep in thought about who could help the girls, the best ways to do it, and what this might look like. I was devastated for them. I opened various web pages belonging to competing news agencies to read different versions of the same news, trying to get that added piece of information as this fast-moving story was developing. Staff started arriving on site to prepare for the many lessons they had planned for that day and the normal chats around the photocopier ensued. They popped into one another's classrooms to borrow something or to touch base. We were a close-knit team. What was very evident about this morning was the way in which the incident in Manchester had rocked everybody. It dominated conversation, and already staff were considering how the children would come into school and their awareness of what had occurred, as well as tormenting themselves with the best and most appropriate ways in which to respond to the children.

I returned to my office, slumping down in my chair, and had my first cup of tea of the morning warming my hands when there was a knock at the door. The knock was firm and unapologetic, and one of my teachers came through the door, asking me if I was aware of events on Facebook. I had no idea what he was talking about until he passed me his phone. There she was. Saffie. A picture of her, with the word 'Missing' above her. As I read on, it was very clear that she too had been at the Ariana Grande concert, something that, prior to this point, I had been unaware of. Saffie was just eight years old and had moved to our school a couple of years earlier from a school in Southport. She was a lovely little girl with an older brother, Xander, who also attended our school and was in Year 6. I knew the children well, having participated in brass lessons with Saffie and her classmates, as well as chatting with them both at the end of most days; very often their parents, Andrew and Lisa (not forgetting Binky the dog), would be fashionably late picking them up, which had become a standing joke.

Here I was, sitting in my office, thinking. On one hand, I had a missing child separated from her family in the aftermath of a terror attack on British soil, with nobody knowing where she was. This seemed an unbelievable situation. On the other hand, I had my team of dedicated professionals who wanted to know what was happening and how to deal with questions from

4

children or parents, and who needed some guidance from me. I was very aware at this stage that I would just have to do what I thought was the right thing, as the time to open the school to the children was fast approaching. I put a message out that there would be a short briefing in the staff room in ten minutes. In the meantime, I would try to establish a link with the family.

I made the call to Saffie's dad, Andrew. The phone rang for what seemed like an eternity, and I was about to hang up when a woman's voice came on the line. She seemed confused, and I asked for Andrew. She responded that she didn't know what was happening. They had lost Saffie and thought that she might have been taken to the Holiday Inn in Manchester, as there had been a lot of children separated from their families after the blast who had been taken there. This was, of course, fake news, but at this point in the day this was the type of information doing the rounds. The reality was that it was just false hope.

As the conversation continued, the lady informed me that the police had just asked to speak to Andrew, and that he couldn't get to the phone as he was with them. Saffie's mother, Lisa, and her sister, Ashlee, were in hospital due to their injuries. It appeared to be quite an uncertain, even chaotic scene on the other end of the phone. I listened intently, trying to glean any information I could. The conversation turned to Saffie's older brother, Xander, with the lady telling me that they were trying to find ways of getting him into school as he wanted to come in for his drum lesson. This at first seemed a very strange comment to make given the circumstances, but fear changes how you think. I reassured her that I didn't expect Xander to come into school, as this wasn't the priority today; we just wanted to know that Saffie was safe and well and reunited with her family. This seemed to have the desired effect and the phone call concluded.

A few years later, I discussed this conversation with Andrew. I asked him who the lady was and told him what was said. He didn't know who the person on the other end of the phone was. I had always assumed that it had been a grandparent, but it wasn't. In such strange and uncertain times, it could have been anyone. A member of the public stepping in, or a family friend who had headed over to Manchester to help in the search for Saffie – who knows?

5

Time pressure was mounting on me to speak with staff, but before I did, I picked up the phone once more. Something in my mind told me that we would need some support as a school, and I keyed in the number of a senior colleague within our local authority, Lancashire. Despite the early call, he was chirpy, as he always was. I described the issue the school was facing and that we had a missing pupil from the terror attack in Manchester. It feels strange to admit now, but, at this point in time, I fully believed that Saffie was alive. I was certain in, fact. The alternative just couldn't be possible: it was too terrible to imagine. I'd been taken in by the fake news and thought she was at the Holiday Inn, hoping that at some point during the morning she would be reunited with Andrew and her family. Perhaps they would turn up in the foyer of the hotel, teary-eyed as they caught sight of her. That feeling of relief, her fears subsiding in her father's arms. I guess some may consider me a little naïve to be thinking like this at this point, but I was. It is a normal human condition to be optimistic. I also didn't have all the information, and certainly not all the correct information. As I concluded my conversation with my colleague from the local authority, I told him that I would be in contact again should the situation change. I was hopeful that Saffie would be found safe and well, but thought that they needed a heads-up, just in case.

My feeling that Saffie was still alive certainly impacted on my approach that morning. I made my way down the long corridor to the staff room, passing classrooms and displays containing colourful work created by our children and painstakingly displayed by the staff. I could hear the rumblings of adult conversations as I walked up the steps and reached for the door, slowly opening it. Silence. Everyone was in there, staring at me, looking for the answer to what we were going to do. I relayed the story of Saffie being lost and the hope that she was safe at the Holiday Inn, but also the fact that we needed further information. Some staff had already heard children outside on the playground discussing that Saffie was missing. Knowing how to address this when they came into their respective classes was a real concern for our team. Locally, this was big news, even at this stage. I set out the plan for the morning, as I thought it was important that our approach was dynamic and easily adjustable depending on what information we received. We would, firstly, maintain a normal morning, as this was important for the children and staff. We would hold our scheduled assembly at 10.30 a.m. for the whole school. At the end of the assembly, we would ask the younger children to go back to class and then address the issue with our older children in Key Stage 2. We would focus on what they had heard, taking a theme of hope, to help them process that one of their friends was missing – a tough ask for a child. In the meantime, should an adult in school be asked about Saffie, they could be honest and simply tell an enquiring child that they had heard that Saffie was missing and that the police would be doing everything possible to find her. The final part of the plan was that we would all meet again during playtime at 11 a.m., to look at where everyone was up to and what, if any, new information was available to us to move forward at that point. The team showed real character as, without further question, they bravely made their way to their classrooms, painting smiles on their faces and feigning normality for the sake of our children.

The early part of the morning following the meeting wasn't too dissimilar to any other, as I stood at the gate welcoming children and families. A couple of parents commented on how terrible the incidents in Manchester last night were and I made polite, non-committal responses. While it was obvious that there was an awareness from some parents that Saffie was missing, nothing was said. Perhaps they had taken the information at face value too? As I moved back inside, I met with my deputy, Janette Higson. She had a grave and worried look on her face, something I hadn't seen before, as usually her bright and vibrant personality shone through in even the most difficult of situations. We discussed different scenarios and what the discussion might look like in the assembly. It was very tough to plan and took a lot of consideration. We were in a forced position where we would have to discuss a terror attack with a group of children from seven to eleven years of age and inform them that, in the aftermath of it all, their friend was missing. Her family didn't know where she was and, seemingly, nor did anyone else. We would tell them what we knew and hope that somebody found her in the meantime.

Those people who know me would tell you that I am not the shy, retiring type. As a class teacher, I had loved and felt privileged to be at the front of the class trying various wacky ideas to embed the concept that I was trying to teach, albeit in a fun and sometimes off-the-wall manner. As a head teacher, I was the same. I loved leading assemblies, getting to see and interact with all the children, while still having the contact and an opportunity to extend their understanding about the world and why it is so relevant to them. But this was different. I dreaded it. As I set the hall up, there was a knot in my stomach – I felt sick. *What music should I put on as the children enter and leave the hall? How will they respond? What if I get it wrong?*

A short while later, the children shuffled quietly into the hall to the sound of Beethoven. After singing a song together, I went about a very normal assembly, using PowerPoint as a visual aid to what I was imparting, and inevitably inviting individual children up to the front to explain an idea or to become part of the assembly. As the assembly neared its end, I invited the younger children to leave, the two blue fire doors closing behind them. There was a real stillness in the large room. I drew a breath: this was it. I told them that a terrible thing had happened in Manchester, a city in their region. There was a bomb at a concert. Their friend Saffie was missing. But, most importantly, I told them about hope. That we needed to stay positive as lots of children had reportedly been separated from their families, that currently everyone was looking for Saffie, and that they would find her soon. You could see the children processing the information. They were deep in thought. I observed them as they left the hall. Many were very quiet and a couple of them hugged staff, including myself, on the way out. They were all heading outside into the playground for playtime. As the last child left, I sighed. Janette was with me, and we concluded that it had gone as well as it could have. As 11 a.m. was approaching, we made our way towards the staff room again for the promised update briefing with staff.

With the exception of the staff on duty, everyone joined us again. I stood, leaning on the side, and we briefly spoke about the assembly. Then it happened. We were all together, and a colleague from the school office stumbled into the room, red-faced and crying. As everyone in the room turned to look at her, she sobbed: 'She's dead.'

Chapter Two

It was one of those moments in life that you'll never forget. Something so big, so uncontrollable, so unbelievable, that it was momentarily difficult to process. After an initial pause, a stillness that felt like hours, people began falling apart. Some were literally on the floor crying, while others hugged each other. This went on for a few minutes. Someone came in, not knowing the horrific news, to see their colleagues, their friends, in total disarray, only to be told the news and then find themselves in the same emotional turmoil. While I certainly would not have wanted the staff to find out in this manner, this was the situation we were all in. I needed to show strength at this impossible time – we all did. I needed to show leadership. Settling the room, I told them that I needed some time to consider the news and the best way forward, and that we would meet again shortly with a firm plan in place. This tactic, on reflection, was one of the most important decisions I made on that day. By buying myself the time to think, I made sure that I was able to do just that – think. This would support everyone better and ensured that I wasn't making emotional decisions that could affect both the staff and children in the longer term.

The staff were simply incredible. I had extended the playtime to ensure we that we had initial time to support one another and that they could get themselves together. They all then went back into class, teaching what they had planned to, in an attempt to provide some semblance of normality – they felt that this would support the children better. To this day, I don't know how the staff did it. They wiped away their tears, washed their faces and simply got on with it. This selfless act of human kindness and focus made all the difference, buying me time to make the phone calls and put support in place.

As I left the staff room that day, I spoke to the member of the office staff who had delivered the message, trying to gain further details of how the information had been relayed to them. We darted into a darkened, empty classroom, where she told me that Saffie's father, Andrew, had called to share the news with the school. Can you imagine having to make that phone call? Can you imagine being the one to receive it, knowing that you have a vital piece of information that is going to turn everyone's life upside down in an instant? It was simply heartbreaking. We moved back to the office.

My first job was to make contact with the local authority. Having failed to get a response, I telephoned my school adviser. She was aware that Saffie was missing, as she had previously been briefed about the unravelling situation. As soon as I had shared the news, she immediately got in her car and headed to Tarleton. This would be uncharted waters for her too, but I was pleased she was on her way, as I had always had the utmost respect for her. She had the right balance of toughness and friendliness you need in a school adviser, both supportive and challenging, as well as having the children of the various schools she supported at the forefront of her mind. Her soft Scottish accent made whatever message she was delivering more palatable.

It was at this stage that I also spoke to Lancashire's CIST team (Critical Incident Support Team). I had, like other head teachers, heard about this team from the local authority. It was they who came to support a school when something really bad happened. It certainly wasn't good news if they were in your school. By the end of the phone call, they too were on their way to the school, with one of them heading down the M6 from Lancaster. It was reassuring that everyone was dropping everything for us.

Soon my office was full, with my adviser and the two members of the Critical Incident Support Team arriving, as well as Janette. We briefed them about the staff response and how the morning had played out. We talked intently about the children and their reactions at the time of the assembly, with notes being taken at every point and careful but silent consideration being made from across the room.

Alongside the pressure that I was feeling, I was also aware that, next door to my own office, the staff in our school office were dealing with an increasing volume of phone calls. This signalled the start of the issues that the school would face with the press. Saffie's name had somehow been released as one of

10

the first victims of the bombing, and this was drawing a lot of interest. It appeared that this was to be a great story for the media, showing the public the human cost of a terror attack. A little eight-year-old girl from a lovely, hard-working family, who had been taken so unfairly and so ruthlessly at such a young age.

The phones started ringing off the hook. A high number of the initial phone calls from the press focused on verifying that Saffie was a pupil at our school. They were persistent in their calls and their attempts to tease the information out of the staff. This was a year prior to the UK General Data Protection Regulation (GDPR) laws coming into place, but already organisations in all sectors were becoming more attuned to data protection, and were preparing accordingly – there was no way that we were going to fall foul of any regulations by giving up this information.

Another, more distressing, issue arose when the phone calls changed their focus. It was probably obvious that Saffie did belong to our school at this stage in the day; we knew this because the press started arriving in droves outside our gates. Frequently, one or another would politely approach the school looking for information, which we declined to comment on. The focus of their phone calls now was to get the home address of the family from us. It is well known now that, at the time, the Roussos family owned The Plaice fish and chip shop in the Lancashire village of Leyland. The village, famous for its truck manufacturing plant, is approximately five-and-a-half miles away from the school. I presume that they had hoped a family member would return and provide them with the photo opportunity – hood up, tears streaming down their face – that they most desired in order to sell a newspaper or two. I still find it hard to comprehend the lengths that some members of the press will go to get this kind of information, as it was clear from the phone calls that some were pretending to be police officers to do so. One also pretended to be a member of the clergy, reaching out so they could support the family. To approach a primary school in this manner, whose priority was children from four years of age to eleven, is morally wrong. We had more important things to deal with on that particular day. It also delayed our being able to give the real police the family's address, as we

11

could then only give that to a police officer in person, who therefore had to come to the school. This isn't something, policy-wise, that we would normally share, but considering the magnitude of the situation, it seemed a reasonable and logical thing to do.

At one stage it felt like we were being totally bombarded. My site supervisor stopped a radio journalist from trying to break into a door at the side of the school. I have always wondered: had he got into the school, what would he have done? It was really very challenging for our office staff, and one of our governors with experience in media relations joined us to field the calls. It was non-stop. Relentless.

The attention started to turn to me. They wanted Saffie's head teacher to come out and confirm she attended the school, and to tell them and the world what she was like. This would certainly help their stories. The requests came from all over the world, and heavyweights such as CNN and the Washington Times wanted to do an interview with me; it was really strange. I had been taught to be cautious. For whose benefit would it be? I made the decision not to engage, for a number of reasons. Firstly, my children, staff, and community came before everything. I was working hard on an initial strategy to support them, along with Janette, my school adviser, and the educational psychologists who formed the Critical Incident Support Team. This was my focus – I didn't want or need the distraction of the media. Then there was Saffie's family. I hadn't spoken to them. I didn't want to speak to the press without first speaking with the family. Inside me, I wanted to tell the world how amazing this little girl was and how much everyone was hurting, how shocked and appalled we were by what had happened. But it wasn't the time; not yet.

On the other hand, my emails had started to ping. Colleagues with whom I was working closely, and some I had worked closely with in the past, had been following the news. It had dawned on them that 'Chris's school' was being affected in such a way. The messages were heartfelt, with offers of support. There were messages of solidarity and hope – many spurred me on with the kind comments that were made. And, although positive, they too were overwhelming.

Like most schools, we have a school Facebook page. It is a great way to communicate with our community and showcase the children's learning and wonderful achievements over the course of a year. It seems common practice for schools to have one nowadays, but at one stage many head teachers wouldn't even consider the use of social media, for fear of an inappropriate post from a parent or perhaps a disgruntled former pupil or staff member. When ours was set up, we wanted to use it as a means of communication and of celebration, but also to promote the fantastic work of our school, as a means of attracting new pupils. It was therefore not set to be a private group and, while only staff could create a post, anyone could comment on it. We, of course, could delete or hide comments if needed. This became important at this point in time, as we received a few comments directed towards me on our page, criticising me for not commenting about Saffie. I vaguely remember one comment from someone in Australia, saying something along the lines of: 'Mr Upton, was she such a bad pupil that you don't want to talk about her?' *Delete.* I am quite a logical person, so an internet troll sitting in a bedroom and goading me from halfway around the world didn't really bother me. They didn't know this little girl. We received a few more, which were quickly deleted, and another positive message with a photo of a fighter jet in a cave, to show solidarity – from none other than the Syrian Arab Army. It was good of them to think of us, but we didn't feel the image was appropriate to be displayed, particularly given the circumstances. I would say, however, that the negative online behaviour did eventually have an impact on both myself and Janette, as we both became obsessed in the coming days and weeks with monitoring people's online responses, in order to protect our community and Saffie's family. This did weigh heavily on us and is probably something to this day that we are still conscious of. We didn't know it then, but social media is an easy means of picking up a story for some journalists. They don't need to walk the hard yards, easily picking up a post and working it rapidly into something: a snippet of news. As the months went on, we would soon notice with clarity that this is what would happen, and events we ran would be mentioned on the radio or in an internet news article almost as quickly as they had occurred.

In consultation with the colleagues in the room, we identified that I needed to make a statement to the press to relieve some of the pressure on the school and my team. I was still struggling, in my head, with doing this without speaking to the family, but there was now such a need to do so that it became an inevitability. More film crews and reporters were outside the school gates. It just seemed like total madness. The local authority was fortunate enough to have an excellent Media Relations team and I worked with a colleague from the team to draft a statement to be released; something they would initially prepare for me to look over. This was all very new to me and, when the statement arrived, I felt that while it did the job and had all the elements it needed to have, I wanted to amend it to reflect the personal link the school and I had with Saffie, an understanding of who she was. I therefore edited it. One of the things that I didn't like in the initial version was a comment thanking people for their thoughts and prayers. While this would have been an acceptable statement to make, my personal thoughts were to steer clear of anything with religious connotations, given the nature of the attack. It was ready to be communicated, and read:

News of Saffie's death in this appalling attack has come as a tremendous shock to all of us and I would like to send our deepest condolences to all of her family and friends.

The thought that anyone could go out to a concert and not come home is heartbreaking.

Saffie was simply a beautiful little girl in every aspect of the word. She was loved by everyone, and her warmth and kindness will be remembered fondly. Saffie was quiet and unassuming, with a creative flair.

Our focus is now on helping pupils and staff cope with this shocking news and we have called in specialist support from Lancashire County Council to help us do that.

We are a tight-knit school and wider community and will give each other the support that we need at this difficult time.

I would please ask that members of the press now give our children the space to grieve for their friend.

I had underestimated how far these words would be carried around the world as they started to appear across the media with my name attributed to them. At one stage, I received a message

14

from a friend telling me that his teenage son had phoned him to say that 'Chris is trending.' I didn't actually know what that meant at the time – all I knew was that I wish I wasn't. Interestingly, the last sentence, asking members of the press to give the children space, didn't get included in many of the articles I have read and was totally ignored. This makes me sad: you have a head teacher openly saying that the children need space to grieve, asking for the press to be respectful, do the right thing and leave them be. They had received this message and had collectively decided not to print it.

While this was all happening, the professional ladies in my office sat with laptops on their knees, either typing emails or researching, with one occasionally making or receiving a telephone call. When you are in the midst of such a situation, you go into survival mode and don't necessarily look after yourself. We were all doing the British thing in a crisis and chain-drinking cups of poorly brewed tea. I hadn't eaten, and the stress and pressure mixed with the caffeine from the tea had given me the most horrendous headache. I was so busy that I hadn't noticed how bad it was becoming. Fortunately, my school adviser noticed I was struggling. It almost seems silly mentioning it, but she went to the local Booths supermarket and bought me a sandwich, drink, chocolate bar and some paracetamol. It really made the difference to me on that day.

It was lunchtime, and the time I had created for myself to think and plan had quickly and suddenly come to an end. I always try my best to keep people in the loop with regard to issues in school, as transparency and openness always win out in the end. I now needed to meet with the staff, to check on them, find out how the children were responding following the distant assembly where we had focused on a theme of hope for Saffie's innocent life, and share the manner in which, over the course of the afternoon, we would answer that impossible question: 'How do you tell two hundred and seventy-six primary school-aged children that their friend has died?'

Chapter Three

As I approached the staff room again that day, I had a small entourage of professionals with me. However, I felt in a very lonely place. The flatness was remarkable as I entered a room of anxious and drained people. In contrast, the large windows overlooking the hot, sunny playground magnified the fun the children were having as they skipped, chased a football, or played a game of tag. Some just sat in the shade to find coolness away from the warm still air, chatting away to friends while making daisy chains, as children had done for generations. It was innocence, beautiful childhood innocence. This would change this afternoon, and for some of them it would affect their lives for years to come, if not forever.

My mind re-entered the room and I introduced the new faces to the school and our adviser, whom everyone knew. We openly talked about the children and how they were feeling. The feedback was positive, as although we were concerned about the children discussing it earlier in the day, the assembly had answered some of their questions and had prompted them to focus on hope, and so they were dealing with the situation well. I then told the staff the plan. I had made a decision that we needed to tell the children straight after lunch that Saffie had died. This was an important part of the plan because I wanted them all to receive the same initial information from a trusted source: their head teacher, me. I felt that this was the best course of action, as unfortunately they needed to be informed, in an age-appropriate manner, of what had happened and to start the grieving process. If the children were to have heard different versions at home that evening, some watered down and some perhaps giving a little too much information, then this could cause problems further down the line. I also wanted to take it off the parents' shoulders; they would find this information terribly difficult to share and might then be haunted by that initial devastation on their child's face. We made further plans around the order in which we would tell the children, and set up additional staff in the classes that we felt would have the most distressed children. We would bring a small group of Saffie's closest friends into a separate room. Janette would accompany me and, should she need to, stay in any class that she deemed needed that additional support. All in all, I would share the news on eleven occasions, with children from as young as four up to the age of eleven.

Additionally, I would send a letter to parents explaining the situation, as they would by now have full knowledge of what had occurred and the presence of the press outside school would clearly be known in the community. They would be concerned about their children, but would be very lucky to get through to school to check via telephone, due to the increased number of calls hitting the office.

The time had come. I chose to start with Saffie's closest friends. This was going to be awful. Prior to entering the room, I had agreed with Janette that I was going to have to keep moving and allow the staff in the room to do their job and support the children as I left, because of the number of times that I would be sharing this horrendous piece of information. This may seem heartless, but it was the only way I could get through it. I went into the room and the girls sat there looking at me, almost as if they were there for something good, maybe a reward or to ask their thoughts on something. I briefly sat down. 'I'm really sorry, but I have some very bad news,' I started. Then I told them. All went quiet, until one of them looked me straight in the eye and said, 'Are you joking, Sir?' I have a strong relationship with the children in our school, much of which is jovial, but this question flummoxed me. I just wasn't expecting it. I looked back at her and responded: 'I'm so sorry, but I'm not. Saffie died last night.' After a momentary pause, there was a terrible noise: a primitive, animal sound that came from the pit of one of their stomachs, a growl. It was chilling. The children didn't know how to respond, and the tears started to flow, as did the sobbing. The staff in the room immediately took over and I had to leave them. Every instinct in my body told me to stay, but I needed to carry on and I needed to trust my team.

Next was Saffie's class. She was part of a mixed Year 3 and Year 4 class, so the children ranged from seven to nine years of age. As I entered the room, Saffie's class teacher stopped the children and they all looked at me. Again, I delivered the news.

17

'You may remember that we talked about Saffie in this morning's assembly. Unfortunately, I have to tell you that she died last night.' Disbelief. Stunned silence briefly ensued, until many of the children started to cry. Again, the staff stepped in. This became a familiar picture as I moved through the school. When I got to our youngest children, something different happened. Apart from Saffie's friends and classmates, I had expected the worst reaction to come from this particular class; some of them were only four years old. I was wrong. They quietly listened to what I had to say before one of them asked me if it was OK to go and play, carrying on with what they were doing before my arrival. It was almost laughable, but it portrayed that childhood innocence once again. What I know now is that they were far too young to be able to fully understand the magnitude of what had happened and was happening. If I had my time again, I wouldn't have visited this class and would have left them to play that day. I felt that telling them had made no impact: put simply, they were too little. On the other hand, our eldest class really struggled with the news. Looking back, it was probably because they could understand fully what had happened and just how huge it was. Someone in their school had been killed. They didn't feel safe any more, because if it could happen to her, it could happen to them. They were scared, really scared. Part of the UK definition of terrorism includes the phrase 'to intimidate the public'. This act of terror was doing just that.

There were two other reasons for their strong reactions. Firstly, one of the children had also been at the concert and survived, physically unscathed. The emotions they must have felt are unimaginable. The second reason was that it was Xander's class. Many of the children were not only upset but also angry. Not only had the attack taken Saffie, but it had also affected their friend Xander so much. Their teacher took the children outside, where they stood quietly in small groups, hugging one another. There was a small number of children with cognitive and learning needs in the class and they found it particularly difficult to cope with the situation. Saffie was a member of our school council and, as such, her picture was on the wall. One pupil took it down and drew on it, not wanting people to see it. This may initially appear to be a really negative behaviour, but it wasn't. It

18

was a coping mechanism. In their mind they were protecting themselves and others from the harsh reality of what was now enveloping them; a viewpoint of 'If we can't look at her, none of this is real.' This, of course, was difficult for the other children, but the staff dealt with it with sensitivity and understanding.

The children in this particular class returned back inside from the playground and their teacher took the lead from them. They were devastated. They drew pictures and wrote letters to both Saffie and Xander, which were later taken to a family friend by their teacher. The other issue staff faced that afternoon was that, as their classroom was at the front of the school, they could see the ever-growing media presence outside. This only added to their fear and confusion, and staff had to stick up large pieces of paper to block out the windows.

Returning to my office, I was uncharacteristically silent. One of the ladies asked how it had gone as I dropped into my chair. It had gone as well as could be expected, and a conversation continued reflecting on what had happened and the children's responses. If I am honest, I put a brave face on it, but I felt broken inside. I should imagine that this was the same for all the staff in the classes dotted around the school, who were bravely supporting the children through this turmoil. Their professionalism was unbelievable.

While this went on, the relentless pressure on the school office continued and, as we approached the end of the school day, the Critical Incident Support Team advised me to make a statement on camera to the press. I couldn't believe that they were giving me this advice at this particular point in time, as I needed to be visible to the parents who had started to congregate in the playground at the back of the school. I didn't listen to the advice given – something perhaps more characteristic of me – telling them instead that we would see how it was in the morning and that I would consider it then. Being there to speak with children and parents was simply the most important thing at that moment. Janette and I headed for the playground.

What met us on the playground was an unworldly silence and a large gathering of people. Every parent seemed to be there to pick up their child; to get that first glimpse of them and check that they were OK. The stillness and discomfort was something that I had felt only a few times before in my life. I had been on a school trip, while doing my A-levels, where we visited Sachsenhausen concentration camp, just outside Berlin. Walking around the remains of the Nazi extermination machine and seeing the most barbaric of human nature, albeit many years after its demise, created an atmosphere of silence, of quiet contemplation, and of fear and disgust. No one talked. And on the playground that day, no one talked. They just stared at us. It was all very uncomfortable, but I understood. They were sizing up how we looked, how we were coping, to try and give them an indication of how their children were. We approached a couple of parents, who expressed their sympathy. The end of the day then came, and with it the doors of the school opened and the children shuffled out, trying to find their parents. It was as far as possible from the happy scenes that I had witnessed at lunchtime only a few hours earlier. Everything was just so flat.

Due to the crowd of press, I had made the decision only to open one gate. The reason for this was to monitor who was coming onto the playground and ensure that we knew who they were. From a safeguarding viewpoint, this would enable us to make sure that everyone got home safely. In addition, it would not have been appropriate to have reporters on the playground. It wasn't appropriate to have them perched at the school gates ready to pounce, but that was beyond my control.

Having only one gate to leave the school from resulted in a bottleneck of people, and an orderly queue formed. It was all rather British. As the children went one way or another up Hesketh Lane, they were approached by members of the press. Most parents brushed them off, seeing it for what it was, but a few stopped to be interviewed or to give their thoughts on the situation, encouraging their children to tell the journalist how sad they felt. This was the angle the press had wanted.

By this point, the local community wanted to pay their respects and, in an area outside the school gates, flowers and tributes had started to be laid. One mother and her little girl stopped to look at them, reading a card, when a female journalist tentatively approached her. I watched the body language of the journalist with interest. She was going to interrupt this reflective time for a mother and daughter, a time that could potentially support the mental health and well-being of this little girl, and she herself was torn as to whether or not to do it. She almost danced on the spot, doing a kind of Irish jig, until her ruthless, professional brain took over and she intervened, sticking her head between the little girl and the floral display in front of her. The girl's mother moved her away, but it was open season, so the journalist merely moved onto her next victim. It was difficult to watch. There were also young people from the local high school walking past on their way home after a day of learning. They, too, seemed to be fair game, and the press relentlessly accosted them, trying to get information that they considered newsworthy. Staff taking children out to get the bus home were also terrorised. It was as if they had gone over the top, entering no man's land, and were in the sights of the enemy. They ignored the questions as they were bombarded, instead focusing on ensuring that the children had their seat belts on and could safely go home. The two staff members then quickly darted back into the sanctuary of the school building, reassured to be sheltered from what was going on outside.

As the last child left the school site, I felt relieved. Tentatively, I made my way back into the school to meet with the staff, as the Critical Incident Support Team were to lead a debrief in the staff room. I was probably one of the last people to get into the room. At least there were some conversations occurring this time. I sat down while somebody kind passed me a cup of tea, thinking that I looked like I needed it. I slowly looked round the room at the exhaustion on everyone's faces, and at the body language in the room, which bore a resemblance to Napoleon's defeated army. Crushed.

The debrief started with a check-in, focusing on how everyone was coping. This was probably standard procedure. It wasn't a question that needed to be asked, but it allowed for people, if they wished, to verbalise their emotions. It then developed, moving on to look at the responses of the children. Reflecting on that meeting, it was all a real blur. What I do remember is just how hot it was in that room, and that those leading the meeting allowed it to go on for far too long. They had lost people. They had lost me. I struggle to sit still at the best of times – my mother believes that if I were a child today, I would

21

certainly have a diagnosis of ADHD. At one moment during the debrief, I saw something out of the window that appealed to my current needs more. A little boy in the after-school club was by himself, kicking a football against the wall. I excused myself, made my way outside and proceeded to have a kick about with him. In all the chaos of the day, this normality, for a few minutes, was like paradise. It brightened his day up, too, and we talked about football. Not bombs, not making sense of dying or press intrusion, just football. The escapism had by then lasted long enough, and I needed to return to the adult world. I rejoined the meeting. It concluded shortly after, and we agreed that the educational psychologists would return in the morning.

During the day, the local community had organised a vigil for Saffie at Mark Square in the centre of the village. The vigil would also be for another victim who lived in the neighbouring village of Hesketh Bank and, at only eighteen, had sadly lost her life in Manchester Arena attack too. It was to be a short event in the early evening that would allow the community to come together and reflect on the lives of these two remarkable young people, and unite us all in our sense of loss and devastation. We had received the invitation earlier that afternoon and, although it would be uncharted waters for all of us, the staff wanted to attend. I think this was a show of solidarity, but also an opportunity to start to grieve more fully, as the focus had been so much on the children.

Driving towards Mark Square, it was clear that the villagers were coming out in force. There was no chance of my being able to park anywhere close, so I ditched my car on a quiet side street, completing the rest of the short journey on foot. Somehow, in the crowd, we all found each other. Looking around, there were a few hundred people, a lot given the space. and a focal point across the car park with a microphone, together with various clergymen who had come together to lead the event. There was a strange busyness, without anything really happening. The press were there too, milling about, trying to figure out who was who. I subtly slipped my lanyard into my pocket. Suddenly, I felt a tap on my shoulder. I was pleasantly surprised to see my wife, Lucy, who threw her arms around me and hugged me. My mother-in-law and her husband stood behind Lucy. It was reassuring to have my family with me, but I had initially not wanted her there. In a phone call earlier in the afternoon I had asked her not to come. This was because I thought I would struggle to look after her, with everything going on and the stifling heat on this relentlessly hot summer's day. Lucy was thirty-seven weeks pregnant and had recently started her maternity leave. I had called her earlier in the day to give her the awful news as it had erupted, not wanting her to see it in the media and start to worry about me. I knew that she would be devastated to hear about Saffie: the attack had rocked North West England particularly badly, and everyone felt a personal connection to it. On top of everything that was happening, you could not help but be worried about someone you love so very much, someone who was carrying your unborn child, especially as seventy-two hours prior to the detonation of the bomb, Lucy was at the Manchester Arena at a Take That concert. Seeing her standing there was a weight off my mind: she was OK, and so was the baby. She probably had a similar feeling as she surveyed me.

The vigil was an important part of the day. It allowed us to step out of the school environment and understand other issues related to the attack, but also to feel a sense of community as we all shared the same horror. Everyone has seen atrocities on the news, but when it is on your own doorstep, it is different. Standing there, it struck me that the purpose of this single act had been to spread fear and separate people, leaving them sad and isolated. However, what I was witnessing, what I was part of, was exactly the opposite. Weirdly, it had brought people from all walks of life together to stand up to terrorism, to those ideals that very few subscribe to. We stood here as one, devastated and angry, but not scared. I've often thought about this, and you see it time and time again when terrible things occur. People come together to make sense of it and to support one another. That is a wonderful thing about humanity.

As the vigil ended, the crowds dispersed somewhat slowly. Small groups chatted, while others moved away. As I tried to make my way from the square, colleagues from other local schools offered their sympathies, and in turn any support that we needed. I briefly spoke with the Bishop, who had led the service with compassion and supported the other victim's family through what must have been an impossible situation for them. Suddenly, I was approached by a French journalist whom I had noticed hovering near me, trying to listen to my various conversations in order to figure out who I was. She finally approached me and asked if I was Saffie's teacher. She probably meant head teacher, but the language barrier got in the way, and so I answered honestly: 'No.' I was Saffie's proud head teacher, but she didn't need to know that.

The end of the most challenging day of my career was almost over. I have no recollection of the drive home that night. At home, I was inundated with messages on my phone expressing sympathy for Saffie's death, but this too, although well-meaning, was again overwhelming, like the emails had been earlier. I made the mistake of putting the news on and remained glued to it for the rest of the evening, thinking about what would happen the next day. You may well imagine that I was exhausted and flopped out in a chair, but nothing could be further from the truth. For that evening and for the rest of the week, I was wired. The adrenaline appeared to still be pumping around my body; I was either on the phone dealing with upcoming issues, or deep in thought, researching various pieces of information, almost detached from it at times. It feels strange saying it, as inside I was deeply affected by all that was going on. This was how I would cope, initially, but it wouldn't be possible to continue in this manner for a sustained period of time.

Chapter Four

Throughout the village, pink and yellow ribbons were flapping in the morning breeze as I drove through, still weary from a restless night's sleep: a colour for each of the two local girls who had become victims of the attack. The ribbons would become a feature in the weeks ahead, and their numbers would grow until most houses had them tied to a gate or a bush; another show of unity. This was the strength of the community that I was serving. As I pulled up to the school, the press were arriving too, getting set up for the morning drop-off. I hadn't expected this, perhaps naively. I had assumed that, by releasing the statement yesterday, along with the press speaking to members of our community as they left the school, this would be enough. What more could they need for their stories?

The children came into school quietly that morning. They seemed to have a nervousness, an apprehension, that wasn't helped by the reporters or cameras in what was a strange situation for a child. I was out on the gate, trying to keep things as normal as possible for the children. That visible leadership was important, and it meant that I was accessible to the parents while also being able to meet the children prior to their entering the building. This meant I could assess the levels of support needed over the day and who might benefit from it. The only issue was that the children needed to grieve. It is part of a child's defence mechanism, so we knew it was going to be a difficult day, but while there would be lots of tears and questions, we would do our best to support them. We were fortunate to have a colleague from another school in our cluster join us for a few days. They had had training in bereavement and were vital in the initial support we gave our children. We were thankful to have their expertise and the support from our colleagues – it meant a lot.

My main focus that morning was bringing the school into our hall, to sing and to fulfil that basic need for togetherness, like any family would do at such a time. We are a community school and, as a general rule, do not pray, as we are a school for everyone. In place of worship, we reflect, we value all, and create open-minded, well-rounded citizens. I therefore wanted to stay true to our ethos and find alternatives to prayer. So we did what we do best, which is to sing. We had deliberately chosen a song that the children were familiar with: 'Don't Stop Believing', by Journey, which had recently become popular again through the television series *Glee*. The message within this particular song was important, and by singing those words, we gained a feeling of togetherness and a sense that we would get through this. The power of music and words should never be underestimated. As ever, the children sang beautifully and with meaning. It was a very emotional assembly and one in which it was OK to cry, regardless of whether you were a child or a member of staff. It was OK to wallow. I stood at the back of the hall, watching intently as I blurted out the words. Some children were comforting one another, in tears with their arms around a friend, while others simply got up, found an appropriate member of staff that they trusted, and hugged them, red-faced. Others were taken out of the hall, not being able to contemplate what was happening yet. Despite the raw emotion, I was pleased that we took this approach. It allowed everyone to physically grieve together, as grief is both physical and emotional. I was also proud of our children. They were showing a superhuman strength in dealing with something so impossible, but within it all, within their own despair, they found compassion and comfort for each other. Not many schools will have had their ethos tested like we have, although there will be some. If I hadn't already worked it out, this was a very special group of children, something that would spur me on in the months ahead.

Later in the morning, we moved outside onto the playground to honour a national two-minute silence, which had been planned to honour the victims of the attack. It was another still, hot day. We assembled all the children and staff in a large circle around the playground. I shared a poem with them, to focus their reflections, and after that we held our own two-minute silence. At the end of the silence we released eight pink foil balloons, one for each year of Saffie's young life. As they silently floated up and away, in a northerly direction, a strange thing occurred: they formed the letter S, before disappearing from view. This may well have been the breeze or some other natural phenomena, but everyone there took it as a sign; a goodbye, perhaps.

Throughout the morning, the relentless pressure from the press continued, with further requests for information and interviews. By mid-morning, the strong advice from the Critical Incident Support Team was that I needed to speak with the press and give them what they wanted. I had still not been able to make contact with Saffie's family, and this weighed heavily on my mind, but I also thought about the staff in the school office and, of course, about our children. I didn't want a similar scene to the previous night, where the press were circling people at home time and filming or taking photos: this was going to do serious damage if it continued much longer. I'd do it. I sat at my desk in quiet contemplation, then opened up a Word document and started to type, adapting the press release from the day before. I knew what I wanted to say. I can't remember quite how, but we had managed to arrange for me to do a piece to camera with one news agency doing the filming for all the other media outlets, then sharing it. This would take off some of the pressure. ITV News were approached and were all too happy to do it. Having put everything in place for an hour's time, I made a telephone call to the local authority Media Relations team. This was somewhat back to front, and took them by surprise. As soon as I had put the phone down, a representative was in his car and heading to Tarleton to give his support, check my statement and ensure everything was done properly. I wasn't sure how I would react if I was given advice on changing elements of what I had written, but when he arrived, he checked it over and confirmed that it was fine. I looked out of the window from the school office and saw a large camera set up at the bottom of the steps outside the school's main entrance. This would make a good backdrop, having the school's name and new logo highly visible. In front of the camera, lots of grey furry microphones were perched, almost in anticipation. It was time.

Don't cock this up, said the minor pep talk in my head as I started to move towards the door at the front of the school. I felt like I was floating. I needed to get a grip of myself; I needed to do a good job. A couple of staff looked at me, almost in pity – Chris was actually going to do this. The door was held open for me and I made my way towards the camera, which had a cameraman and a journalist standing behind. These were the real professionals. They were respectful and knew what they were doing, seeming to understand just how difficult this was. It was a lonely place to be standing. Like most head teachers, I didn't have any media training, but here I was. I needed to be a professional, too. Drawing a breath, I said the following:

News of Saffie's death in this appalling attack has come as a tremendous shock to all of us and I would like to send our deepest condolences to all of her family and friends.

Saffie was simply a beautiful little girl, in every aspect of the word. She was loved by everyone, and her warmth and kindness will be remembered fondly. Saffie was quiet and unassuming, with a creative flair. Saffie comes from a close, loving family, and we can only imagine what they are going through.

It is hard for adults, let alone children, to grasp the unfairness and utter randomness of this terrible act. Our job now is to support our children and families to deal with the after-effects of this traumatic experience, and we are being supported by a specialist team from Lancashire County Council in doing this.

This morning, we came together in our hall as a school community, where we held a minute's silence in Saffie's memory. We then sang, 'Don't Stop Believing'. As you can imagine, there were many tears from the children and the staff, but we know together we have to hold onto the love among us; we owe that to Saffie and her family.

I would please ask that members of the press now give our children the space to grieve for their friend.

With that, I turned and moved back into the safety of the school. I wasn't asked any questions, because we had agreed that it would be a statement only. I had tried to do it on my terms, to give them what they wanted, and hopefully this would work, releasing some pressure.

Having watched it back in recent years, I can't believe that I forgot to put my suit jacket on – something I should have done, but had slipped my mind.

The clip of Saffie's head teacher, standing outside her school, telling the world who she was and how much she would be missed, went all around the world. I was conscious of my own family in Jersey seeing it, and called my dad to explain that I had just read a statement out regarding Saffie and that I was being advised that it would be on all the major news networks. They, too, were following the events intently, and I didn't want my face coming up on the news to come as a surprise to my mum and dad. Like any mother, she would be worried about me, so it was only fair to give my dad a heads-up.

Cards started to arrive at school, as did the very many emails I was receiving from all over the world, expressing sympathy for the children, staff and Saffie's own family. Saffie had really captured people's hearts, and we had become the epicentre for that outpouring of grief. The public, strangers, were struggling to come to terms with this little girl's tragic death. There were many people who contacted me from across the globe, including from America and New Zealand, as in the past they had lost a child or a young relative. Their wounds had been reopened and they wanted to reach out to the school and the children, as they knew what a terrible ordeal they must be going through. This was meant with the best intentions, but at times on that day, and for some years that followed, it was challenging. One gentleman travelled via bus all the way from Manchester, coming to the door to deliver a card. This was well meaning, but he then wanted to use the toilet. I felt awful, but there was no way, with how the staff and children were feeling, that I could allow a stranger into the school. So I politely directed him towards a supermarket down the road.

I received letters from schools up and down the country, as well as those from the world of education, including one from the well-known educator and writer Dame Alison Peacock. One letter that really stands out was from Russell Hobby, then the president of the National Association of Head Teachers (NAHT), of which Janette and I are members. It wasn't his kind words and offer of support that stood out, but the fact that it was handwritten. This doesn't happen often nowadays. When did you last receive a handwritten letter in a professional situation? It really was a touch of class and something I will take forward, as I know how it made me feel at that moment. Janette received a similar letter and shared my sentiments.

The children were really struggling at this stage. Nearly all of them had come into school, which we believed, as their parents did, was the best course of action. There were many tears still, and an unfamiliar quietness around the building. They were frightened and we were struggling to reassure them, given the situation. We tried to keep things as normal as possible, but were guided by the children, and would take opportunities for discussion, supporting them either as a whole class, as groups, or as individuals. This was a decision we made internally, as a school, as the short-term support from the Critical Incident Support Team, who had come back to the school on the second day, was almost over. Their support was running its course and I felt it had been somewhat limited. In fairness, I had probably expected more but, given the situation, this just wasn't possible. In terms of their support, what had worked well was the information and knowledge they had provided; for example a CIST leaflet that went home to parents to accompany my letter, explaining what had happened and what their child had been told. We had considered inviting parents to come into school and providing tea and coffee for them, giving them a chance to talk and ask questions. The CIST team reflected on this with us and helped us to reach the conclusion that, due to the intrusiveness of the press, the end of the day needed to happen swiftly. They had recognised the burden on staff answering telephones and had suggested the press statement, which was impactful. They reflected on what happened and made some suggestions, as well as the staff debrief on the day the news broke, but that seemed to be it. I had received a very long email of reflection, but it was difficult to read and take in, as I was emotionally full. I didn't see the value of it at the time, although re-reading it years later I could see that they were trying to help me. I am quite a practical person: if there is a problem, let's put support in and get it fixed. We were from different worlds. Sometimes you need really practical things, boots on the ground, and these were not being sourced for us. The hardest thing for me to accept was that, at times like these, we initially couldn't do this as we needed to have 'a period of watchful waiting as children and staff move forward through the tasks of grieving.' At the end of the second day, the two members of the CIST team, both pleasant and polite people, left the school. And, despite a couple of exchanged emails, that was the end of the support from the local authority, with the exception of our school adviser, who checked in regularly. As they walked out the door that day, our 'specialist support' was over. We were by ourselves. I discussed this with our school adviser many months later, and the feedback from the CIST team had been that I wasn't responsive to them: they had pushed it back onto me. Covering yourself is very common in local authorities, and I wasn't surprised by this response. Maybe they were even correct, but a one-size-fits-all approach in such uncharted waters isn't always the answer, and I knew that I had a strong team. By hook or by crook, I would just have to go out there and find the bespoke support we needed.

At home time that day things were less intense, but the press continued to be a problem. By now, the more reputable press such as Sky News or the BBC had been respectful and left us to get on with our business. It was the international media that had camped out for the children and their families on this particular afternoon. I remember the hilarious scene of our lollipop lady stepping out into the middle of the road to stop the traffic, with a French cameraman filming her. He followed her every step by standing opposite her, like he was her mirror image. Her voice, with its Lancashire accent, called over to me, 'I'm not being funny, Chris, but this is ridiculous!' They just didn't seem to care. The Russian journalists were the least problematic: they stood without movement, watching. But there was an Italian crew who were a real nuisance, getting in people's way and repeatedly asking me for an interview, which I declined. The reporter was overfamiliar which was not well received on my part. What made me sad was that the staff wanted to go out to the front of the school to look at the floral tributes and read the very many messages and cards which had been left. We didn't want to give the press that photo opportunity, so we watched and waited until they had left for the day, then we all went out together. I think the scale of the situation really hit many of the staff at that moment. After two days, they were running on empty, as the initial adrenaline was almost gone and the effects of sleep deprivation were kicking in. It was good to have that short moment together.

The following morning, I pulled up at school, only to be greeted in the car park by the friendly Italian journalist. Again, he tried to persuade me to do an interview. He was literally begging me. He struggled to understand why I wouldn't do it. Unfortunately for him, my patience was gone. I was in a place where I had had enough, so I looked him in the eye and told him in no uncertain terms that I wouldn't be doing it and that that was the end of the matter. All the frustrations of the last few days were close to erupting. I just about kept a lid on it, telling him that he needed to get his car out of the car park before I shut the gate and he would have to wait all day to get it back. With that, I marched inside to calm down before the children got on site. It wasn't my finest hour as a head teacher, but we are all human, after all. Fortunately, that was the last time I had to speak to him: he'd got the message. I found out later that morning that, prior to our little set-to, he had chased other members of staff across the car park as they made their way into the school. It was appalling. My team was focused only on supporting the children that week and just needed the space to do so.

What troubled me the most that day was that a couple of Year 6 boys had arrived at school, upset by the press. I saw them approach me, perhaps in a belief that I could do something. They said, 'Sir, please will you just make them go away?' The children had had enough, too: it wasn't fair. Although there was little I could do, I knew that there was light at the end of the tunnel, as it was the Friday before we broke up for a couple of weeks' holiday. What a shame that, in a country such as ours, a head teacher cannot protect against the emotional abuse of his pupils. Such is the power of the unregulated media.

Breaking up for what was a two-week half-term holiday was a double-edged sword. On the one hand it allowed everyone to take some time and space to support their own recovery, but on the other, perhaps it would have been better for us to stay together a little longer so that the support was there. Alongside the emails, letters and cards we were receiving, there were lots of different types of support being offered to us. Professionals local to our school offered services such as counselling for free in the coming weeks and months ahead. I wasn't in a position to respond to these yet, but really valued the kind offers, particularly as we were without what I perceived to be practical support from the local authority. I decided to create a simple table, as due to the sheer volume of correspondence I was receiving at this time, it would have been easy to lose their details, which could potentially have an impact on future provision for our children. One example of support from this list was from a counsellor called Colin Butterworth. Colin lived a couple of villages away and, due to his background and qualifications, reached out to the school. When the time was right, I made contact with him regarding support for the children who were most in need. Colin was incredible over the two or three years that he supported our children, refusing to charge the school, which was probably to his detriment. He ran individual and group counselling sessions that took the lead from the children. He had a natural manner with them, and they opened up to him, sharing their scariest emotions. Colin would have been a similar age to their grandparents, which I think helped too. His soft Scouse accent and occasional open question put them at ease, supporting their recovery.

Prior to the onset of the half-term holiday, I had one last favour to ask of my school adviser. So many Lancashire colleagues had been in touch. Some I knew incredibly well, others by name only, and there were some I hadn't heard of. So many had taken the time out of their busy days to put pen to paper or to send an email to share their thoughts and prayers with us. There were so many that I couldn't respond to them all, but I had a solution to this. The local authority use an internal online portal for messages and information sharing, and this would be the perfect place to put a message, in order to thank everyone in one go. It was really important to me, in the middle of everything, to be well-mannered and grateful for the support we were being given from afar. I therefore contacted our school adviser and, of course, she made it happen, which really supported me. The following message was placed on the Lancashire Portal:

I would like to take this opportunity, on behalf of our school community, to thank Lancashire colleagues for their tremendous support following the tragic events that led to our beautiful Saffie-Rose leaving us on Monday night.

We have received messages of support across the county from so many people, many of whom I have not met, and they have helped get us all through what has been a very challenging week. I have asked to put this message on the portal as responding to everyone would be a challenge in itself.

The support we have had from a variety of people from LCC has been first class, and we are proud to be a Lancashire school. Having such a strong local authority, with such a wealth of experience, really makes a difference to children's lives in good times and bad; long may it continue!

Please join me in raising a glass of something, during your well-deserved half-term, to Saffie-Rose, our little Lancashire Rose.

I had written the message on the third day after Saffie had died, and while my opinion would change in respect to the support from the local authority, it was important to note that individuals had tried their best for us.

On that particular Friday, we had also realised that it would be wrong to close the school without offering any support for the following week. It would have been easy to lock up and simply disappear, hiding in a dark room, but this wasn't how we did things. I had been provided with contact details for Child Action Northwest (CANW), which is a commissioned service supporting young people's well-being in a variety of areas. With the bombing being the main news at the time, they were happy to help. I was very aware that it wouldn't be young people just from our school who might be struggling, so we set up a drop-in event with CANW, based at our school, and used our networks to let people know what was happening. On the Tuesday of the first week of half-term, four counsellors from CANW came into school, setting up in a classroom each. Members of the local community could come into our school and confidentially meet with a counsellor. I had asked if any staff were available to be on site with me to support the offer and in my error had left this as an open invitation. It was an error because so many staff turned up wanting to offer their support. Other people also came; another adviser from the local authority, for example, simply to check in on us in her own time. Lucy, too, had come in and joined office staff in collecting some of the cards from the floral tributes before laminating them and putting them back outside to protect them from the forecast rain. They were really going the extra mile.

Two ladies nervously appeared at the door. I greeted them warmly and they introduced themselves. They were Saffie's former teachers from her previous school, Kew Woods in Southport. I was really touched that they had come to see us, to check in on us and join us, which they did for a short time. Saffie's death must have been so difficult for those ladies, but also the other staff at their school, as it hadn't been long since she was wearing their school uniform.

Everything was positive on that day. There were only a small handful of families who accessed the services we had put on, but that was OK. People were still coming to terms with everything. I knew that if we had helped one person, it was worth doing. Then, with one phone call, things turned sour. The ladies in the office were upset, as a member of the press wanted answers to his questions - when they hadn't given them to him, he had become rude and obnoxious. The next time the phone rang, I took the call. An arrogant, sorry excuse of a man was on the other end of the phone. He demanded the name of my staff member, before telling me that the school should be open throughout the holidays in case a member of the press needed information. From this last comment, it was clear to me that he wasn't going to get very far. I turned the tables on him and told him that I would like to make a complaint about his conduct and asked what his name was and where he was calling from. He told me that he was called Gabriel and that he worked for some media company. The highlight of his response and the entire conversation was that he went on to tell me that he wasn't answerable to anyone; he was the boss! I wasn't going to win an argument with him; he was so self-obsessed and lacking morality that I figured out simply putting the phone down on him would upset him much more. I had a vivid image of him stamping his feet as he smashed his phone on his desk. As the phone immediately started ringing again, for added effect and to protect the office staff, I asked them not to answer any more calls that day. They were then off for quite a few days. We never heard from him again.

Chapter Five

The imminent arrival of a baby should be such a happy time, and in some ways, it was. Lucy was merely days away from giving birth, and we were both relieved to have some headspace afforded to us by the half-term. Being pregnant can heighten emotions and Saffie's death had hit Lucy hard, as too had her obvious concern for me and the stress and pressure that I had faced. Like many feeling Saffie's loss, Lucy hadn't met her, but everything was just so close to home and she couldn't help but feel devastated for Saffie's family. This was a real worry for me, as her husband, so I tried to put a brave face on things. I think it would have been any reasonable person's go-to to find a pub and sink a few drinks as means of escapism for a couple of hours. This certainly would have been my solution, but I couldn't, as I had to be able to drive in case we suddenly needed to make a mad dash to the hospital. In its place I decided my best solution would be to cycle to a pub, grab a pint, and then cycle home past the canal again. I would still be able to have a beer and the exercise would do me good. It would give me time to think while ensuring I could get home quickly if needs be, and didn't mean being away from Lucy for too long. It probably sounds selfish, but there were points, over that two-week period, where I needed to be alone, to cope. It goes without saying that I knew that particular strip of the Leeds Liverpool Canal very well indeed.

One of my main concerns remained: I hadn't spoken to the Roussos family. This had always impacted on decisions I had tried to make with issuing statements to the press and, now that I had given such statements, I was worried that I had perhaps upset them somehow without meaning to. This was really playing on my mind.

I'd had enough. I couldn't sit here anymore, worrying about things. I needed to be proactive and find out for myself. I had been glued to the media coverage and had become aware of a family spokesman called Mike Swanson. I found out that Mike had a computer shop which was situated just round the corner from the family's chip shop. The weather was appalling, and torrential rain hit the car windscreen as I made the short drive to Leyland. As I got out of the car, the wind whipped up too and, by the time I could see the chip shop in the distance, my clothes were saturated. Not really knowing where Mike's shop was, I walked around the area until I saw a sign for SOS Computers. It was a small shop with bits of equipment dotted about, but clearly there was a larger area at the back of the store where the repair work was completed. A tall, skinny assistant asked politely how he could help. I asked to speak to Mike and the man seemed a little reluctant. It then dawned on me that they too must have been bombarded by the press and he wasn't sure who I was. I offered that information freely and he disappeared to make a phone call, I presumed to Mike. Moments later he came back out to the front of the store with a very different demeanour, one of warmth and friendliness, explaining that Mike wasn't there but was on his way. He asked if I could come back in twenty minutes. I had little choice but to venture back out into the storm to try and find something to do for twenty minutes. The problem was that there wasn't much to do so, having missed lunch, I located a Greggs and settled on eating a sausage roll to kill a bit of time. I daydreamed, looking through the condensation that fogged the large glass window, as I ate quietly in the corner, sheltering from the storm. Were there going to be an uncomfortable few minutes ahead?

To my relief, as I nervously entered the shop for the second time, Mike was there and greeted me, saying, 'Well, I don't need to ask who you are!' He put me immediately at ease as he gripped my hand firmly. We had a lovely conversation and I told him my concerns about upsetting the family. He almost laughed at me, telling me not to worry, and that Andrew Roussos had been touched by what had been said. I cannot express my relief – it meant that I could sleep that night. Mike and I exchanged numbers before I left, asking him once again to pass on my condolences. Through reaching out, I had managed to make that contact which, I didn't know at the time, would be important in the many months ahead in planning events and liaising with the Roussos family. For now, I was just pleased to have had some contact.

During the half-term, like most head teachers do, I continued to pick up emails. This was an important time to monitor and communicate, as there continued to be many people wanting to make contact. We even attempted some normality as a family, with the odd day out: I recall a game of crazy golf with my two sons from my previous marriage and a very heavily pregnant Lucy, who was simply glowing as she moved around the course. I was there in body and sometimes in spirit, but at times I found it hard to fully engage with my family, as my mind could easily drift. Then it happened. Through all of this, Lucy went into labour, and one of the most magical experiences of our lives occurred: the birth of our son Arthur. My mind was focused again, and I was in total awe of him and of Lucy.

Arthur was born the day before the start of the second summer half-term break and, although I was on paternity leave, given the situation there was no way that I would be able to simply switch off from work for two weeks and pick things up again thereafter. This just wasn't an option. Fortunately, I have a very supportive and understanding wife, and together we made this work. I would be at the end of the phone for Janette, I would pick up emails, and would sort anything that needed to be sorted. It was all such a rollercoaster of emotions. The guilt I felt for not being front of house leading the school was terrible, but good leadership reflects the systems you set up working when you are not there. I was, of course, tinkering away in the background. I also felt guilt for being happy – anyone would have expected me to feel happy at the arrival of our son, but in the midst of this, of seeing families lose their children, their loved ones, and with the close proximity of Saffie and the Roussos family, I felt it. I know now that this would have been the last thing that Andrew and Lisa would have wanted me to feel at this time. Perhaps being in the background, work-wise, for a couple of weeks would be of benefit to help me focus and respond better when there were issues that needed to be addressed.

Two days into the new half-term, three days after Arthur's birth, I received an email from a concerned governor with regard to a local decision for the removal of the floral tributes from the front of the school. From the email, there appeared to be a slight tension in the village about who was making decisions, and it was their viewpoint that some locals were getting ahead of themselves and almost becoming unofficial spokespeople for the school. This was not an opinion I shared with them, as we were very careful about our communications. It was a brave email, at that point, for our governor to send. They raised the issue directly with us and I appreciated the heads-up – after all, everything linked to the village and the school at this time was so emotive. I did, however, agree that the floral tributes should be moved. This was incredibly difficult. Around the country, there are decaying floral tributes tied to trees or bridges, perhaps with a football scarf or shirt tied to them, remembering the last place a particular person drew breath. In terms of the floral tributes outside the school, they had served a purpose in that they had allowed the community to share their outpouring of grief and to show the children, staff, and school that we were all loved and in their thoughts. At this stage it was three weeks since the bomb had gone off, and we needed to seriously consider the impact on the children of coming to school each day and seeing a decaying tribute. We were also hoping that Saffie's brother Xander would return to school in the coming weeks. This was no longer cathartic for the children, and would not support their recovery or Xander's return. I spoke with Mike as the link to the Roussos family. The community had a simple solution, which was to move the floral tributes from the front of the school to the village centre, Mark Square, which was just under a mile away. Mike confirmed that the family were aware of the situation and were happy with this solution, as they too were in agreement that this arrangement would support Xander. A short and to the point letter was needed, to quash any issues, and, as Janette was at the helm, I put one together for her so that she could focus on the children. It read:

Dear Parents/Carers,

I am writing to provide reassurance to our community regarding the removal of the floral tributes from Hesketh Lane in front of the school. There have been some reservations regarding this.

Firstly, the school have not removed them. This has been done by members of the community who have relocated them to Mark Square. I can confirm that this has been done in consultation with the family through the family spokesperson, whom I have also had a conversation with.

The family have been greatly touched by the warm support of the community and are happy with the new location of the tributes.

The school's main focus is to continue to support its community, and in particular Saffie's family. It is important to recognise that we all grieve differently, and I hope that this letter has addressed any concerns.

Yours sincerely
Chris Upton

The letter was effective in that it stopped any further issues in what could have been a rather difficult situation for the school. Nobody complained; they were now accepting of what had occurred, probably because they were reassured that it was a solution that the family were happy with.

We have all experienced seeing people grieve, and the initial support of the nearest and dearest of the deceased person. Everyone is shocked and everyone is available to lend a helping hand. While this cannot go on forever, there is a small window where it is very prevalent. I have often sat in funerals, thinking about the widow sitting at the front of the church or crematorium, and thought, *You're soon going to have to go this alone.* And while there is some support, it is inevitable that you will have to try and make sense of your life and adapt to your impending loneliness like so many others have before. As a school, this would be slightly different. We were about to enter the window of support, which was always well-intentioned, but was almost certainly random. The world had left us alone in the first week of half-term and, not knowing that we had a second week where we would also be off, the emails started on that Monday.

The first wonderfully random thing was about to happen. I had initially received a phone call from a lady called Rhiannon. She worked for HarperCollins Publishers as a publicist and had an author who wanted to visit the school to help cheer up the children and take their minds off what had happened in Manchester. He had been moved by the story and, like so many people, had a genuine concern for our children. His name was David Walliams.

The correspondence between Rhiannon and myself went back and forth. I had rejected the first date that was offered because we had our annual Sports Day scheduled and I didn't want to disrupt the parents who had taken time off work. Looking back now: what was I thinking? It was David Walliams, and I probably should have just gone with it. However, in my mind at the time, it was important to provide stability for the children wherever possible. There were many details in the preparation for David's visit and Rhiannon was obviously accomplished at her job, leaving no stone unturned. It was a wonderful thing that David was doing, but I think, from the precise details in the various emails, he was nervous about saying or doing the wrong thing, and he sought absolute clarity on the small details which would ensure the event's success. We settled on a date in late June and made a decision to keep it a secret. There were two reasons for this. Firstly, we didn't want any press involvement. We hadn't seen them for a few weeks now and this was better for the children. Secondly, we needed a boost. This would surely help us to put a smile on our children's faces.

The day came and we received a copious amount of boxes with books in them. Generously, David was going to give two books to each child in the school: *The World's Worst Children* and *The World's Worst Children 2*. This was incredible for the children, but he didn't stop there. David provided two copies of every book from his backlist for the school library, and would sign each copy when he arrived at school. Rhiannon had got to the school an hour before David was due, to ensure that everything was ready in the manner he wanted and would run smoothly. The hall was set up with a chair in the middle of a stage area for David, and then chairs on each side of him where our school council would sit. This created a slight V-shape, with a small table in the middle where Rhiannon arranged some books for use in the assembly, Post-it notes poking out of them so that David could quickly navigate to a page mid-flow. Behind this loomed a large screen that was to be used to project images. David had asked that each of the children be given a question to ask him as part of the performance that he would give. Prior to the assembly, I had spoken to the children involved, telling them a little white lie that I was doing a special assembly and that I was going to dress up and pretend to be David Walliams. This really wasn't outside the realms of possibility, given some of my assemblies, and all the children took the bait hook, line, and sinker. We were also very aware that we didn't want any of the staff missing out. As we had gone incognito, I told those not working on that day that we were having a special assembly and that I would really appreciate having everyone there – they all came.

About an hour before the assembly, I told the ladies in the office, as there would be no way we would get past their stealth senses. Sworn to secrecy, they were very excited. We got everyone into the hall and another member of staff led a singing practice, just to keep them busy and to allow David to find his feet. A black Audi with tinted windows drew into the car park, pulling up at the front of the school. There he was: it was David Walliams. It was all rather surreal. I welcomed him into the school and the first thing that struck me was how tall he was, as he stood there in a suit, no tie, extending a hand for me to shake. What was very obvious, as he muttered his condolences, was that he was nervous. I hadn't expected this. David has a wonderful persona that audiences around the world enjoy on their television screens, but in person he was very different. I was a little nervous too, and we all went to my office, as you would want any guest to the school to feel relaxed and welcome.

Within the office, we sat chatting as he started to sign some books. Rhiannon went through the final arrangements. David showed great concern for our children, asking about how they were getting on and talking about the assembly so that he didn't say anything that might cause offence or set us back. He was a professional who had come here to lift the spirits of the children, and was making sure that he did just that. We talked about the last couple of weeks and he explained he had become aware of the school through the media. I told him of the issues that we had had with the press and the impact on the staff and children as a consequence, telling him of the relentless pressure on us and some of the more negative press behaviour that we had experienced. David listened intently and reflected that he himself had had difficult times with the press: unfortunately, as a celebrity, you came to expect elements of this, but as a school in these circumstances it was wholly unacceptable. I couldn't have agreed more.

Rhiannon looked at her watch: five minutes to go. Then David asked me a question, in his rather posh voice. He had been on a train for a number of hours and then straight into the waiting car at Preston train station, and so he said, 'Could I use your bathroom?' This was a reasonable request and at any other time it wouldn't have been an issue. However, there was one very big problem with this: the gent's toilets were located right next to our school hall, which at this stage had around three hundred unknowing people waiting for some sort of 'special assembly' to start. There was no way that I could let him use them, as it would have spoilt the surprise. This was awkward and I had to think quickly on my feet. I smiled politely and explained the predicament. In those few seconds, I had figured that he could use one of the children's toilets. I would check they were empty first, as the children were in the hall, then stand guard outside to ensure nobody came in. I relayed my plan to David who, after a moment's reflection, replied, 'I quite understand.' Off we went, with the very tall David Walliams…and some very low toilets. It was all fine and David was as gracious as ever.

Moving through the blue double doors into the school hall, I could see everyone was there. It seemed packed. I was so excited to see everyone's reaction and to see if we could pull this off, keeping the secret right up until they had this wonderful surprise. I had only come back off paternity leave a couple of days before, so this was my first assembly in a few weeks, the first since we had joined together and sung 'Don't Stop Believing'. The children seemed pleased to see me and I started the assembly. I told them that I was really tired: Arthur had been up all night and my cats Ziggy and Blue had been causing a nuisance. I went on, 'I'm too tired to do this assembly. Would anyone else like to do it instead?' Lots of hands flew up and I asked again: 'Anyone?' A familiar voice rang out across the hall, and David Walliams burst into the room, making his way towards me, saying, 'I'll do it!' It was priceless. The children and staff sitting on benches almost fell off in shock, while the other children gasped and hugged each other in excitement. They simply couldn't believe it. There was probably no better person to have in our school hall at this exact moment in time: he was a famous children's author, with our children reading many of his books; he was a judge on *Britain's Got Talent* and other shows – they simply adored him. As he approached me, he high-fived me and took over. To the children, I must have looked like the coolest head teacher of all time. I joined them in order to enjoy the assembly. He was fantastic, answering questions and reading excerpts from his books, with a highlight for the children being the story of 'Windy Mindy'. It was brilliant, and as I sat there enjoying the assembly, my attention turned to the children and staff, and I watched them momentarily. They had been and were going through an impossible situation, but seeing them enjoying the assembly showed me that there was hope. We would need to plan plenty of opportunities for good times ahead, and that was OK. Saffie had died. But, more importantly, she had lived, and we needed to focus on this more in our recovery.

Following the assembly, David returned briefly to my office, where he finished signing the last of the books and kindly gave my eldest two boys, who were huge fans of his, a book each, signing both. I couldn't thank him enough for what he had done, and he will probably never know how important his visit to Tarleton was to our school. Not only had it raised everyone's spirits, but it had also given me lots of thoughts about leading the school through a period of recovery in the months ahead.

Although we had not alerted the press to David's visit, inevitable articles followed the visit and I am sure there may have been some frustration that they didn't get a photo opportunity. But the visit was about cheering up the children. One article that frustrated me was in one of our local papers, the Lancashire Evening Post, with whom we normally have a positive relationship. They had made contact with a representative from the talent agency that David was signed to and gained the following quote:

A representative of Troika Talent Agency, which represents Mr. Walliams, said: 'David gets contacted by lots of schools asking for a visit on his book tours, and although he tries to get to as many as possible, he usually doesn't get much further than

London because of his other commitments. But when Tarleton contacted him, he wanted to make a special trip, after they were affected in the Manchester bomb attack. He spent some time with the children and read some books. I think he really enjoyed the visit.'

The thing that really bothered me was that it was being reported that we had made contact with David Walliams. This simply wasn't true, as we had been approached via email by his publicist at HarperCollins. I felt that, not only was it untrue, but it could also potentially appear that the school was attempting to profit from Saffie's death, something that troubled me endlessly, especially as this could have upset her family. People will call it semantics, and it didn't appear to bother anyone but me. However, it was wrong, and either the paper had reported it incorrectly, or their source, this mysterious representative of Troika Talent Agency, had given the wrong information or had chosen their words carefully to manipulate the situation. Ultimately, we had been honest and true and accepted a kind invitation in the spirit of helping our children – this was my goal, and I needed to let this go as it probably wasn't going to get me anywhere, just pull me off my stride. Another issue the Lancashire Evening Post's article had made me consider for the first time was that the press were monitoring our school Facebook page, and were able to use very basic posts and information to turn them into an article.

The next randomly wonderful thing came about a week after the visit of David Walliams, in early July 2017. I was sitting in my office, working at my computer with Janette, trying to get some semblance of normality back and create a strategic plan for the year ahead in September before we went off for our well-needed summer holidays. An unexpected email popped up in my inbox. By this stage, I had received so many weird and wonderful emails from all over the world that it looked like spam. Not taking much notice, I nearly deleted it. However, a quick glance at it changed my mind. I read on intently, stopping what we had been working on. Janette instinctively asked me what it was and who it was from. With a dry smile, I turned the screen to face her, asking her to read it for herself. Her eyes darted quickly from line to line and, when she was finished, she sat back in her chair, deep in thought, before saying, 'Hugh Grant, as in *the* Hugh Grant?' She studied my face for a response, which came with a gentle nod of my head. Her reply was hilarious, and one many women may have had: leaning forward, she gripped my arm, and with what was almost a demonic stare, she uttered the words, 'Can you get him here?' I exploded into laughter, which was very quickly replicated by Janette, and I told her to behave herself.

The email from Hugh Grant was as big a surprise as it was warmly appreciated. It was strange, receiving an email from someone who, as a famous actor, also had a very famous and distinctive voice. When you read the email in your head, that clear, upper-class English accent would take over, leaving you in no doubt who had written it. After some pleasantries, it became clear what the reason for the email was. Hugh wrote, 'I just happened to bump into David Walliams the other day, and he mentioned that while he'd been visiting your school you had mentioned that you had had some trouble with press intrusion.' The email went on to describe his involvement with the organisation Hacked Off. The Hacked Off campaign had been set up in 2011 following the phone-hacking revelations in the media at the time. As an organisation, they support and work closely with victims of press intrusion and continue to respond to issues in this area, in what many consider is a fairly unregulated sector. Hugh's email opened the door for us to share our experiences and take any relevant advice from those who understood the press.

I responded to Hugh straight away. There were two reasons for this. Firstly, someone as famous as Hugh Grant had bothered to make contact. It was strange and almost flattering that he and David Walliams had had a conversation about the school and, from that, he had tracked down my email and made the approach. Quite simply, he didn't need to do this, but this random act was important to us and, from what Hugh had been subjected to by the press over the years, was obviously something he was passionate about. This was not only for himself but, with his in-depth understanding of the issues, he wanted to help others. The second reason was that I felt I owed it to our children, staff, and school community to at least have the issues around the press during that terrible week in May looked into. It was also important that we shared these events, to hopefully stop instances like this happening again. I think it is important to remember that the aftermath of the Manchester Arena attack did see a shift in what certain elements of the press considered fair game. It has been well documented that families of victims were approached before knowing that loved ones had died. The use of individuals' social media accounts to track them down by the press was rife. Requests for further information in an attempt to obtain them from sources, such as the attempts to get the Roussos family's address by pretending to be police officers, were happening to lots of people. This was all a real game-changer after a major incident, and technology was supporting the press to behave in such a manner.

Following the initial exchange of emails, Hugh put me in contact with Daisy Cooper, who at the time was Hacked Off's Joint Executive Director. A couple of years after receiving her help, Daisy went on to become the Member of Parliament for St Albans. Daisy was incredibly supportive, and we set up a telephone call during the last week of the summer term. I found her incredibly easy to talk to and it was clear that, despite her warmth, she was an accomplished professional, asking the right questions to elicit the details she needed from me. I talked her through my concerns about the press and the impact it had had on our children. My view was and still is that there should be a greater protection for schools and their pupils from the press, as they are a place of learning. Children should not have been sitting in classrooms, in what was already a traumatic time, worrying about walking past a crowd of press in order to simply leave the premises and go home. There was also consideration of the staff, particularly those in the school office who were taking the telephone calls. I think that the link with Hacked Off really supported me on my journey as a leader at this time. As the head teacher, when everyone's back is against the wall, you want to protect them and do the best by them. Talking through things with Daisy helped me to offload, but also to gain a sense of perspective on everything. She was level-headed and helpful. We discussed the high volume of phone calls hitting the office from journalists and broadcasters. While she was sympathetic, acknowledging that the team would have felt bombarded, she also felt that the press had a legitimate interest in Saffie's death as a news story.

Daisy sent me a summary email a few days later which initially acknowledged this part of the conversation, but also acknowledged the key areas where she felt more 'devious behaviour had occurred'. This included finding a person trying to break into the school through a side door, who claimed to be from a radio station; people whom we believed to be journalists telephoning the school pretending to be police officers and asking for the home address of the family; and finally, the aggressive phone call during the half-term break, asking why the school wasn't co-operating with the press and demanding that we open up. On the latter point, she had tried to track down this person, but had drawn a blank and it was therefore not obvious that this person existed. Daisy reflected that the behaviour in question was concerning, but without hard evidence that these were all in fact journalists, we wouldn't be able to report the behaviour. The advice that Daisy gave would be that, should a parent or child be approached again, they would need to get all of that journalist's details and make a complaint should they feel harassed. This would be unlikely now, as we were a couple of months down the line, but I appreciated what Daisy had done for us as a school. Although in terms of the media, little would change in the near future, at least we had logged it with Hacked Off. We had had it looked at and were provided with the correct and impartial advice that, while frustrating in parts, allowed us to move on. Daisy left the door open to get back in contact should we need it, and I was grateful to both Daisy and Hugh for their help and for taking the time to support us.

Chapter Six

The third wonderfully random thing to happen also came via email. It was from a gentleman by the name of Peter Heginbotham OBE. Peter was making contact on behalf of the Japanese Embassy and had the official title of the Honorary Consul for Japan in Manchester. Within his email, he explained that a non-profit organisation called the Kids Earth Fund had been in contact with the Japanese Embassy. They were an organisation that worked worldwide to promote peace and environmental conservation through the medium of children's arts. When the Manchester Arena attack had occurred, Japanese children wanted to show unity with British children, and they had produced a number of artworks. Reading the email, it struck me again that the attack had been so pointless. From across the world, this was another example of people connecting, of children connecting: we were all being brought closer together. The email went on to explain that seventy of the paintings had been donated to the embassy to be displayed for one week, after which they could be donated to an appropriate school. Peter felt that we, in light of Saffie's death, would be that appropriate school and that he would be honoured to donate them to us.

Receiving this email wasn't what I had expected when I got up that morning. However, it was lovely to receive, and before sending a reply to accept the offer, I considered what the children and staff would make of it. I was sure that at first it would seem a little strange, but it was a lovely gesture.

Responding to Peter, I firstly apologised for the lateness of my response, explaining that I had just come back from my paternity leave. Peter seemed a lovely and kind man, from his warm response. He may well have had the nervousness that David Walliams appeared to have had on making that first contact with the head teacher of a school that was grieving in such a way, not knowing what the response, if any, would be. I was a little unsure about how best to proceed with gaining the pictures, so took the lead from him. We agreed that he would come to school with his wife, Margery, around the middle of

July, quite near to the end of term. They would bring the pictures and present them to our school council, who would look at them and then ask any questions.

The day came and I had prepared the children for what was to happen. The concept of an embassy is a tricky learning point for primary-aged children, so it took me a little while to try and explain this – I was probably not very successful, as there were many blank faces staring back at me. They were excited, though, as they knew about Japan and they wanted to see the pictures. I knew that our children would receive our guests warmly, as they always did, and that I could rely on each and every one of them. When Peter and Margery arrived, I invited them into my office for a cup of tea and a chat so that I could orientate them to the school. We could finalise what was about to occur and hopefully listen to and take away any niggles or last-minute concerns that they might have – this was a learning point I had made from my encounter with David Walliams. I would now always assume that visitors at this time would be stepping into the unknown and could feel uneasy or nervous about saying or doing the wrong thing, potentially causing upset. That was never going to be a problem, and we chatted freely before we made our way down a corridor to meet with the children, who were waiting in a spare classroom.

You never know how even the most confident adults will talk to and relate to children, but Peter was a natural. I imagined he was probably a wonderful grandfather to some loving grandchildren somewhere in the North West, and he spoke to our children enthusiastically about the paintings and his role. He showed them the artwork, and the children were quite struck by them. They all had a theme of peace, but it was the style that really stood out. There was no doubt that they had been beautifully created by Japanese children, as there was a real Manga flavour to them and they were completed in chalk. The children reflected that some of the images reminded them of the cartoon Pokémon. They were poignant too, some having both the Japanese and the Union Flag on, depicting the message of unity for which they had been created. Watching the children intently, some of whom were Saffie's closest friends, this really meant something to them, and it wasn't causing them upset, but instead was helping them. They were totally involved in the moment and the pictures. What a wonderful idea the Kids Earth Fund had had, and I wondered whether or not a similar impact had been seen after other disasters around the world, where a simple piece of artwork, a token of humanity, meant so much. At the right time, these pieces would be useful in our recovery, and the cogs began to whirl in my head with lots of different ideas.

Before Peter and Margery left, we all went into the central garden at our school with the children and took some photographs of the visit, along with some of the pictures, as if Peter was handing them to us. The weather was beautiful and just perfect for this lovely and most productive visit that had supported our children and their early recovery well. I talked to them about an idea to exhibit the pictures, and they were keen to come back, should we ever do such a thing. They would certainly be at the top of our list to invite. Both the children and I had enjoyed their company. I thanked them as they left.

Moving back to my office, I uploaded the photos and set about creating a Facebook post about the event for our parents and school community. I hadn't really considered at this stage that it would have wider appeal. But half an hour later, my Chair of Governors arrived for a pre-scheduled meeting and, when I mentioned the visit to him, he told me that he already knew because he had heard about it on a local radio station. It appeared that our social media was again being monitored and that our information was quickly being used to create stories linked to the school and, of course, Saffie. Having been aware of this following the visit of David Walliams, I had put that particular article down to being a one-off. What this now told me was that what was happening at our school in the aftermath of Saffie's death was all still very relevant to the press, and that they could now get what they needed from a distance. Naively, I had been giving it to them. Personally, I just saw it as lazy journalism and found it quite odd, but it drew my awareness to the fact that we would need to be careful with what we posted and would, in the coming months, need to consider that what we were posting could be manipulated into an article by different areas of the media.

From the very many cards and emails we received from around the world, one thing was very evident, and that was that the condolences were not just from adults. A significant amount of the outpouring of grief and love was from children. Saffie's death had really affected them. She was a little girl of a similar age, and she had died. This was frightening to children, some of whom would have been at a developmental stage in their life when they realise that they themselves will die at some point, something I remember well from my own childhood, after awakening abruptly from a dream about a coffin. The Manchester Arena attack was such a big story that children across the country would have seen it and known all about it. Seeing Saffie's picture and hearing her story would have affected them. In their minds, a little eight-year-old girl had gone to a concert and been killed by a bomb that had also injured her sister and her mum, leaving the latter in a coma. It couldn't really get any worse, could it? No wonder these children wanted to reach out to the school, but more specifically to Saffie's friends.

Cards and pictures from our neighbouring schools came quickly, as they too felt the shock that resonated through our local villages. These were lovely to receive, and further messages came from other schools, too. Prior to taking up the post at Tarleton, I had worked in the Lancashire town of Skelmersdale or Skem as it is more affectionately known locally. As a head teacher in Skelmersdale, I had been very involved with the local education scene and had many friends still there, having worked in the town in various schools and roles from the onset of my career, spending eleven years there. The messages from these schools poured in. The children of these schools wanted to do something to support our children. They held non-uniform days, they prayed for us, lit candles for Saffie, and many schools raised money that they gifted to us to help our children in the weeks and months ahead. There were many schools who did this, and a substantial amount of money was coming into the school, leading to our setting up a memorial fund. Schools were donating hundreds of pounds, mostly from the non-uniform days, which were child-led. One school donated £1,800, a vast amount of money.

I received one message from a teacher at a school in Birmingham, who explained that she had led a circle time discussing the tragic event with her class of seven- and eight-year-olds. This must have happened up and down the country as children tried to make sense of what had happened. Their skilled teachers would have found the right words to convey what had happened in order to support them; a difficult task, but one expertly done. This particular class had wanted to do something to show their love and support for the children of Tarleton Community, particularly Saffie's classmates, whom they wanted to make feel better. They had therefore created a beautiful mural from natural resources, which included the word 'united' made out of sticks.

Another school, located in the valleys of South Wales, had a group of pupils who were so saddened by the events in Manchester that their Year Seven children requested to write letters of support to our school. Reading the letters from these young people was incredibly moving, as they wanted to reach out to us and innocently express their feelings about the hopelessness of the situation, another reminder of lost childhood innocence. One letter read:

'I am deeply sorry for the loss of your student Saffie-Rose. I have a cousin around the same age as her and I know I would be devastated and would struggle if I lost her. So, stay strong. We and the whole country support you and Manchester. Stay Strong!'

These letters really reflected the mood of children around the United Kingdom during that snapshot in time and they, like the adults, put themselves in a position of loss, in the position of the Roussos family, and it was unimaginable. It was a wonderful gesture, and articulated a coming together of children.

Something rather spectacular had occurred in the North East of England. I first became aware of it from an email, entitled 'A random act of kindness from the city of Newcastle'. It was from a gentleman by the name of Craig Heeley. At the time, Craig was the vice principal of Hilton Primary Academy in Newcastle upon Tyne. His pupils had also been affected deeply by the Manchester attack and the death of Saffie. In the days of the aftermath of the attack they had gone to the city centre and handed out various cakes and treats to cheer up members of the general public, some of whom wanted to donate money to them. This was inspired by an episode of the popular BBC children's news programme *Newsround*, and by Saffie's story. There was a pattern here. Again, from many miles away, strangers, children, were reaching out to us. The email read:

Following the tragic events at Manchester Arena on 22nd May, our Year 5 children discussed what they could do to change all the negative emotions people were experiencing back into positive ones - they decided to plan a 'Random Act of Kindness' that took place at the Monument in our city on Friday 26th May, where they handed out free cakes, cookies and sweets to members of the public.

As the children contacted local businesses in the build-up to the event and shared it with our community, it became evident that people wanted to donate money in return for the act of kindness. Following a discussion with the Y5s and watching Newsround, we were all very touched by the story of Saffie. The children decided that they would like to donate any of the money raised during our random act of kindness to the classmates of Saffie, to put a smile back on their faces.

The day itself blossomed into something quite beautiful. Stagecoach put on a free bus for the children to get into the city centre; we'd had donations from various local shops, bakeries, etc. Members of the community had baked cakes for the children to hand out. When we arrived at the Monument there was significant media coverage of the event – they'd picked up on the event from our social media feed.

To cut the story short, our children managed to raise in excess of £2,000 that day from the people in our community and the city of Newcastle. How you spend this money, we really don't mind, as long as it puts a smile back on the faces of your kids & community.

The video itself went slightly viral on Facebook and we were touched when we received comments from members of your community (parents and a teacher at your school!)

I cannot begin to understand the emotions you and your community will be going through at the moment, but as a final 'act of kindness' myself and a few of our children would very much like to come and present your guys with the cheque at some point when you feel it appropriate (Alternatively, we would love to host yourself and some of your children in Newcastle if you would prefer).

I know that you'll be extremely busy at the moment, but I look forward to hearing your reply.

Best wishes from us all in the North East.

I watched the clip on the BBC News and was in awe of the children and how they had brought their community together. It was also clear that the attack had rocked communities up and down the country in the days and weeks following it. It had created a sense of terror. I liked Craig instantly; he had turned something so awful into something positive for his children. He and his colleagues had been brave, taking a risk and doing what was right for their children. Their moral values were being developed and the public engaged so beautifully with them – they were lucky children to attend such a forward-thinking school. Responding to Craig, I initially had to put the brakes on, because we were still on half-term and I would need to assess how the children came back to school. There was no way I could lead a jolly up to Newcastle, although it did seem rather appealing. Craig understood and I left it with Janette to deal with. Emails bobbed about between the two schools over the weeks of the summer term in order to arrange a visit.

Eventually, Craig, a colleague, and four children did make it to Tarleton. It was September 2017 by this stage, which worked better for us as a school as we simply couldn't have coped with visitors any sooner. This small group of Geordies travelled around 150 miles via train to spend just a few hours with us and to present us with a very generous cheque for £2,000. The children joined Saffie's classmates, and I recall watching them all chatting together. They struggled with each other's accents, but the smiles and laughter showed that they were forming new friendships. Saffie was bringing people together yet again. The few hours passed and it was time for us to transport them back to the train station in nearby Preston. I wasn't sure how the visit would go and was intrigued to find out, but it had been brilliant, and our children really appreciated it. All those kind words and well wishes from after the attack had been summed up in this one symbolic visit. It also enabled our children to reflect that, although a few months had passed, people still cared about and were thinking of them and of Saffie. This was important to our children. I thanked Craig profusely as we stood on the steps at the front of the school, shaking hands. It had been beneficial to both schools.

Like the children, the impact on adults and on those in the education community was equally significant. People were putting themselves in the position of the family and how they would feel if they were Andrew or Lisa Roussos, losing a child. It was all very close to home for everyone, myself included. The responses I received from around the world were incredibly emotional; it was difficult initially for me to know what to do with them, and perhaps to understand that raw emotion from strangers. One person wrote, 'I am struggling with knowing what to write as tears are welling in my eyes. My daughter is only five, and as a parent these events really hit home.' These weren't isolated messages from parents around the world, as more and more followed, either landing in our inbox or through the post.

Other messages came, relating to personal experiences of other terror attacks that had occurred in the years prior to 2017 and the Manchester Arena attack. One message came from a retired medical professional from the state of Colorado in the US. They referenced the work they had done in the aftermath of the Columbine High School massacre in April 1999, where two students had gone on a shooting rampage, killing ten fellow students and shooting a further twenty-one people before turning the guns on themselves in the school library. They had also made a number of bombs, which fortunately had failed to detonate. At the time it was the deadliest high school shooting in US history. This person had an enhanced understanding, as a professional working in the aftermath of an attack, and her words drew parallels between both incidents. They wrote, 'Both groups acted cowardly against unarmed and innocent children. We are sickened by what you are going through.' Reading messages like this made me feel sad that others before me had dealt with such difficult situations, but worse that people following me would also have to do this, due to someone's sick ideals, and that families and children would be affected for the rest of their lives.

The other messages came from the world of education, many from head teachers or principals, but others came from high-profile figures such as Vicky Beer CBE, the Regional Schools Commissioner. While many knew me, many did not. Talking to colleagues in the years that have passed, I think it was the image of me in my pink shirt, standing outside the school, reading a statement to the press. They will have had huge amounts of sympathy for what we were going through as a school, but equally a relief that it wasn't them. Over the years, I have spoken to a couple of members of the press who were at the school on that day, and both separately reflected that they were shocked by the behaviour of some of their colleagues from other agencies. When they witnessed me speaking about Saffie on the step, they both had a feeling of 'that poor bloke' and 'rather him than me'. In making that comment, they were aware of the press, or should I say elements of the press, swarming the school off-camera, ready to pounce on anyone they could lay their hands on. Other head teachers could put themselves in my position: professionally, it was their worst nightmare. The emails and cards came from the length and breadth of the country. From Sandbach in Cheshire to Cornwall. From London to Scotland. Again, it was overwhelming, but incredible in the same instance. One message from a head teacher in Nottinghamshire read, 'I wanted to send you and all your community my support. I cannot imagine how difficult today must have been for you and everyone else. Please know that you are held in the thoughts of everyone in the country.' We also received messages from companies that we did business with or bought resources from. There were messages from wider family members of children from our school, uncles, aunties and grandparents of our children, who lived all over the country and who wrote to me to express their feelings and to connect. It was difficult to take in at the time; too much, really, and I wasn't in a place where I could take it all in. I had to continue to do the best for the children and staff, so I had to push all these kind thoughts and prayers to the back of my mind to focus, I mean really focus.

The strength of our local community also shone through at this time. We started to receive donations, which was the catalyst for our setting up the memorial fund – something that we had not even thought about, but the donations came in so thick and fast that it was a necessity. I was approached quite early on by one of our dads. He wanted to set up a fundraising concert to celebrate the lives of the two local girls who had been victims of the attack. He was very experienced in this field and, as we discussed the possibilities of such an event, it was clear that another wonderfully random event was in the offing. He had a number of contacts who would support him to get a stage, the technicians, and the artists to a venue in Tarleton. He also had a friend who would headline the concert – he was the one and only Chesney Hawkes.

Sitting in that meeting was very surreal and I wasn't really sure if it would all come together, if I am totally honest. There were many barriers in the way, the most obvious one being the venue. We could have held it on our school field, but there would have been issues with parking and the size of the site, so we really weren't an ideal choice for it. Tarleton Academy is our local high school, to which a vast majority of our children transition as they leave us. They were approached and quickly agreed to host. I think it is fair to say that in hindsight, this decision probably caused them some regret, something that I cannot blame them for. Certainly they may not have gone ahead had all the barriers been known to them: there was a lot of red tape. We supported them by agreeing to hold the money raised in our school fund, before writing cheques to the agreed recipients, who were the two families, Runshaw College (where one of the victims had attended), and ourselves. The red tape resulted in a much smaller audience than had been originally planned for. However, it would be a community event to celebrate the lives of these two young people, and what more fitting way than in the form of a concert. The One Love, One Voice concert was set up and ready to go. It was planned and impressively set up in only a few weeks; a testament to the hard work and dedication of the dad and the team at Tarleton Academy.

In early July 2017, the concert took place. Our school choir had been asked to perform at the concert, which was fantastic, because not only did it allow our children to be part of something, it also allowed them to creatively express themselves. We have a wonderfully talented choir who sing beautifully and who, during the summer prior to this, had won a regional singing competition. At the One Love, One Voice concert, they had a green room which in its real function was the academy's sports hall. The children loved this, as they had their own section with a rider of an assortment of treats. It also allowed them to mingle with the other performers backstage. They were lovely with our children, the most accommodating being Chesney Hawkes, who went out of his way to talk to the children and settle their nerves – he was really accomplished at this. He stood chatting away to staff and children in jeans and a khaki T-shirt, long necklace hanging from his neck, wearing a light brown trilby hat. While he was much smaller than you would have imagined, he didn't seem to have aged since he was catapulted to fame in 1991 in the title role of the film *Buddy's Song*, alongside The Who legend Roger Daltrey. Chesney's hit 'The One and Only' was taken from the soundtrack of the film and lasted five weeks at Number One. Chesney had his wife and children with him that night, and came across as a lovely man who was a dedicated professional, and also someone who was a natural in front of a crowd, commanding a stage and audience with ease.

Elsewhere backstage there were random stormtroopers stretching and doing backflips in an effort to warm up for their part of the show. This was, of course, an act known as Boogie Storm. Boogie Storm had been contestants on the widely popular television show *Britain's Got Talent* a year earlier in 2016, and had made it to the final, coming a respectable third. Dressed as stormtroopers from *Star Wars*, they were a dance troupe who had caught the nation's attention and admiration with the complexity of their dance sequences and athleticism during their performances. By not speaking with the judges, but maintaining the anonymity of being stormtroopers, this had also created a mystery to the act. The children were incredibly excited to see them, as they would all have watched them on television and known who they were. Sadly this probably wasn't the case for Chesney Hawkes, who was more of their parents' generation and, of course, mine.

The singer Kevin Simm was also performing at the concert, as he had grown up and still lived fairly locally to the area. Kevin had initially been in the pop group Liberty X in the early Noughties, but had made a comeback on the television show *The Voice UK* and had won that particular competition in 2016, a year prior to the concert. This meant that he was again well-known to the children and they were excited to see him. He also made time for them, and this was lovely to see. Alongside these well-known singers and performers was a local teenager called Ethan Cross, who was an incredibly talented singer and who would revel in the opportunity to share the stage later on in the evening. Finally, a young singer by the name of Henry Gallagher completed the line-up. Henry was known to the children, as he had been involved with the Last Choir Standing Competition that the school had won the year before. Subsequently, they held a celebration at a restaurant owned by one of the parents. He had been booked and had come and played, much to the excitement of the children, who they felt like they knew him. Henry was an up-and-coming, talented musician, and had initially come to the public's attention in 2015 on *Britain's Got Talent*, singing a song called 'Lightning' about a girl he was too scared to ask out. The children simply adored him.

There was a real buzz in Tarleton that evening, something that had been lacking in the weeks that followed the bombing. For once, the stillness had gone, as the local community made their way along Hesketh Lane to the academy with a cool box or camping chair under their arm, holding hands with eager children who skipped happily next to them. As I arrived with my eldest son, I could see the stage with barriers protecting it, and a few tents and fast-food trailers dotting about. I think that it is fair to say that it wasn't as big an event as was first imagined, due to the bureaucracy involved, but it would serve the community well in its response to what had happened in May. There was a high profile of security and, as I was fortunate to have a parking space on site, I was stopped and had to show my ticket and identification to proceed any further. Security was key to the success of the event. This was so close in time to the Arena attack that people were fearful; this was a real first step to recovery, so having that reassuring presence in the village was vital that evening.

Looking back now, the whole concert was a relatively brave thing to do on what was only the forty-sixth day after the Manchester Arena bombing. There would have been those who didn't come because it was too soon. In agreeing for our children and choir to be part of the concert, I had taken this into consideration. How would they cope? Was it too soon? I was of the view that it was a different situation and was in their own community. Having been an amateur musician myself, playing in many bands and orchestras growing up, I understood how performing live could make you feel ten feet tall, with the endorphins rushing around your body – our children needed desperately to feel this. Of course, performing on that evening wasn't a three-line whip, and it was always at the discretion of our children's parents. However, we as a school would prepare them, and this was something we did. The proof is always in the pudding and, as Duncan Heather, internationally acclaimed vocalist and compère for the evening, introduced the first act, the Tarleton Community Primary School choir, the crowd erupted. They were with us. The children nervously shuffled onto the stage, their talented teacher, Mrs. Russmann, in front of them, smiling and settling their nerves with every glance. Her hands were raised as the audience fell silent and the music started. They sang. They sang beautifully and, with every word, seemed to grow in confidence. I felt so proud of each and every one of them, knowing in this instance that this had been the right decision. It was escapism in the moment. They finished singing and everyone was on their feet. They stood there, happy and astonished. I think it was the community's way of directly showing our school how much they thought of us, our children, and that they were there. It was an incredibly powerful moment for those children.

The rest of the concert continued and the children were now able to relax and enjoy it with their parents. I milled about and spoke to a variety of people, some I had only recently met over the last few weeks, including Mike, the Roussos's family friend. It was a wonderful evening. Chesney Hawkes was headlining the concert, and as such was the last act to perform. As one of the most famous one-hit wonders on the planet, we were all waiting for that one song from him. When it came there was a roar from the crowd, with many of us joining in with the lyrics of 'The One and Only'. All the performers, with the exception of our school choir, came back onstage and sung the Oasis hit 'Don't Look Back in Anger', a song that had become an anthem and sign of unity in the aftermath of the attack. There were video messages too, exclusively recorded for Tarleton's One Love, One Voice concert.

Celebrities such as Amanda Holden, Olympians Jessica Ennis-Hill and Beth Tweddle, as well as the pop group Union J, had all recorded messages of solidarity for our community. This again strengthened the feeling of support from around the world on that evening. Finally, Ariana Grande's management company had granted permission for the use of the artist's video of her performance of 'One Last Time' from the One Love Manchester Concert that had occurred a month earlier. This served as a poignant reminder of why we were there.

The evening had been a great success, for many reasons. It had brought the community together and allowed them to show the world a togetherness at a time of fear and great sadness. It had given some of our children the escapism that they needed and the understanding that everyone was still there, something important in their grieving processes. It had also raised around £8,000, which would be split between the two local families and associated education institutions, and this would go some way to supporting all concerned in the weeks, months, and years ahead.

Saffie's ninth birthday also fell in July. We held a Wear What you Like day, with children and staff wearing blue or green, Saffie's favourite colours. The children found this a difficult day, and we had to put a lot of support in place. Away from school, an event had been planned in Leyland, in the street where Saffie had lived. Many of us went over to the town that evening, to what was a birthday party for her. It was quite remarkable what had been put together in such a short space of time by the other shopkeepers and friends of the family. The people of Leyland really did Saffie proud. There were fair rides and stalls. People were celebrating her birthday and her life. It wasn't a sad occasion, but a positive one for those children and their parents who had come across. I took my family with me and we enjoyed it. It was nice to see people outside of the normal school context and be able to chat freely with everyone.

Chapter Seven

A few weeks after the bombing, I had had my first conversation with Saffie's dad, Andrew. While the initial conversation was never going to be easy, probably more on my part, having that nervousness of trying not to say the wrong thing, I was also relieved to speak to him. I wanted to know that he and the family, but most especially Xander (who at this time was still a pupil at our school) were OK, or as OK as they could be given the circumstances. We were all relieved when Lisa, Saffie's mother, awoke from the induced coma she had been placed in due to her injuries, having been standing with Saffie when the bomb was detonated. Andrew had been through hell and back, and was still living it. The death of his much-loved daughter in such devastating circumstances; supporting his beloved wife, Lisa, while she was still in a coma; and then having to find the words to tell her what had happened to Saffie; being there for his stepdaughter, Ashlee, who had also received injuries in the blast; and finally, being there as a dad for Xander, to help guide him through what was a new world, at a time where he should be excitedly transitioning to high school. The plates Andrew was spinning were unthinkable to anyone else, but he had no choice: he had to carry on.

The children in Xander's class had struggled over the course of the term, as Xander hadn't come back into school. They missed him, and just wanted to see him and know that he was OK. Over the weeks this became the focus of their questions to their teacher and to other adults in the class. She didn't have the answers for them, which made it more difficult. Xander never returned to our school; with everything that was going on, he needed to be with his family. There was, however, one last chance for him to see his friends, and this opportunity presented itself on the final Year 6 trip, which was a visit to the local bowling alley. This was two months after the bombing, and must have been so difficult for Xander, who came with his characteristic smile on his face. The fact that the children had already started bowling was useful, as they were in smaller groups and this meant he wasn't overwhelmed. The children were excited to see him, but there was that initial awkwardness, which soon melted away. This was a hello and a goodbye, although they probably didn't realise that at the time. This final meeting was important for the class's recovery, as the confusion and anger about what had happened to their friend had now been present for many weeks. This had affected some children's behaviour, and some of the children were in a low mood. They were kind, thoughtful children who just wanted to make it better for Xander.

In my role as head teacher of Tarleton Community, there were practicalities that would always need to be dealt with professionally and with planning and forethought. Good leadership is about considering potential barriers. One issue that I needed to consider over the summer term was Saffie's funeral. Due to the nature of Saffie's death and the high-profile status it had taken, we weren't sure when it was going to be. Slowly, the funerals of other victims began to take place. There was the obvious initial issue for the Roussos family, which was that Lisa was in an induced coma. Her recovery would then follow, to physically get her in a place where she was able to attend her daughter's funeral. Finally, there was also Saffie's family in Cyprus to consider. They needed to get over to England and have a place to stay. It must have been incredibly challenging for the family to plan. In terms of the school, we would have considerations of our own. We very much expected the funeral to take place on a school day, which would bring its own issues, the main one being: should we shut the school? This may have been a dilemma for many head teachers, but I had absolute clarity in my mind around this. Yes, of course we would shut the school. The vast majority of staff would want to attend the funeral to pay their respects and, should any of our parents want to attend with a child, they could do so. This was potentially going to lead to a clash with the local authority, with someone telling me I shouldn't have done it, as had been the experience of other head teachers in the past, but I was happy to take one for the team on this occasion. I firmly believed that it was the right thing to do, and my governing body would have stood shoulder to shoulder with me. To mitigate any impact on our parents whose children may not have been as closely linked and who didn't want to attend the funeral, I had a discussion with the executive leadership of Tarleton Academy. I asked in principle if they could do anything to support us, on this hypothetical day, for any children who may need it. They were well-placed as they were very local to us, and were also the home of the West Lancashire Sport Partnership, who led sport at the local primary schools, including holiday camps. In my mind, we could put together an activity day, should we need it. I was thankful that, in principle, they would support us, and we agreed to talk around the finer details as and when there was further clarity on the situation.

As we moved towards the latter end of the summer term, phone calls between Andrew and I became more frequent. We both updated each other on various issues and touched base. This is something that still occurs to this day. Generally, Andrew will send me a message to see if I am free, then I call him when I can. I think this developed through Andrew not wanting to go through the office to speak to me, avoiding the well-meant questions about how he and the family were that, while well-intentioned, are difficult to answer when your world has been destroyed. I would have done exactly the same in his position.

On one such occasion, in July 2017, I received a message from Andrew. Calling him back, he updated me on the funeral details. The funeral for Saffie would be held at Manchester Cathedral on Wednesday 26 July. Her funeral would be in the first week of the summer holidays, therefore the issues of shutting the school had eroded. Unbeknown to me, he was about to ask me something that would not only be one of the most challenging things I had ever done, but also be one of my greatest honours. In Andrew's customary matter-of-fact way, he asked me if I would give the eulogy, or tribute as it is more commonly known nowadays, at Saffie's funeral. I accepted in an instant. How could I not? It was going to be really difficult, daunting, in fact, but I knew that I would be able to hold myself together on this occasion and help to celebrate the life of this wonderful little girl. In a small way, I wanted to be able to represent the thoughts and feelings of her family, friends, and teachers in reflecting to the world just who she was, who she could have been, and just how loved and important she was to everybody.

To do a good job on the eulogy was vitally important to me. I had a limited number of days to research, write, and then practice it, to ensure that it was delivered at Manchester Cathedral in a confident and polished manner. It needed to be personal, too. Saffie was one of my pupils and I was feeling her death just as much as anybody else. I am pleased to say that nowadays a eulogy is more frequently delivered by someone who knows the deceased, but this hasn't always been the case. I recall sitting at my grandfather's funeral, listening to the vicar talk about my grandad; but he didn't know him. The essence of who my grandad was, in my opinion, was missing. There weren't those joint experiences and stories, for example him terrifying a police officer by waving his walking stick in their face when they wouldn't let him go down a street. Or the time when the exhaust pipe from his new car had fallen off on holiday, due to him ramping the car off small bridges at high speed to impress me, his devoted grandson. He had then turned to me and muttered the immortal words, 'Don't tell your grandmother!' If I was going to write a tribute for Saffie, I would need to meet with the family, so that all of her short but precious life could be celebrated. I picked up the phone again, calling Andrew, and made the arrangements to come and visit the family. It would be just me, a pen, and my jotter, things that are never far away from a decent head teacher, although some now prefer to use technology such as an iPad. For me it is pen and paper all the way. I'm a little old-fashioned that way.

Lisa had been recovering at Wythenshawe Hospital, just under ten miles from the Arena and close to Manchester Airport. The family had been provided with a bungalow on the hospital grounds, to live in while Lisa recuperated. She had many appointments each day and therefore needed to be on site, but also needed to be around her family. They all needed each other. Wythenshawe wasn't an area that I was particularly familiar with, and I had left school slightly late – I have a habit of never leaving myself enough time, something that distresses Lucy, who is always on time. It was quite a journey from Tarleton, and, on this occasion, I would have to rely on my ageing satnav. Needless to say, it failed me somewhat, but after a couple of three-point turns I was at the hospital gates and was able, from then on, to follow Andrew's instructions to find their bungalow. I parked up and made my way to it. Andrew was outside and greeted me warmly, with a slight smile. I returned the pleasantries and made my way over to him. What should have been a handshake, wasn't. We were both beyond that after everything that had happened, and I hugged him. They didn't teach you that when I did my qualifications for headship, but it felt right.

Moving inside the bungalow, I saw that other family members were sitting in the lounge area. They all seemed genuinely pleased to see me, with the exception of Binky the dog, who studied me inquisitively before barking at me and being extradited to one of the bedrooms. Lisa came in, in a wheelchair. She looked in such a bad way, and was in obvious pain from her mental and physical scars. However, when we started talking about Saffie, she lit up and I knew that the old Lisa was still there.

It was important, touching base with the Roussoses. I needed now to sit with them and listen as they shared all those thoughts and memories of Saffie. It was a really intimate meeting and I was privileged yet again to be part of this storytelling, in what was essentially an outpouring of love for their daughter. One thing I wanted to do was to take them back to when Saffie was very little and hear the tales of her as a baby and as a toddler. There were wonderful stories; every family has them. Those little moments that would mean little to anybody else, but when you talk about them, something in the pit of your stomach glows. I heard tales of Saffie's early life in Cyprus, dancing at family parties to the adoration of all the adults in the room. Of her fearlessness, something that featured throughout her life, including, as a toddler, climbing up onto Andrew's Harley-Davidson in a shop owned by the family. There were also stories of the interactions and love between Saffie and her siblings. Her grown-up sister Ashlee would take her out on exciting excursions and she would play the part of the annoying little sister to her brother Xander, putting yoghurt pots in his shoes, forever the wind-up. That didn't stop at Xander, as she would also wind up her beloved dog, Binky. Sitting there, scrawling almost illegible notes, there was no doubt in my mind that it could have been anyone, any family. They were just like any of us, and in a cruel twist of fate, here they were, recalling the life of their daughter.

It was strange, hearing them all, and I reflected to myself that I was starting to know Saffie better in death than when she was alive, which upset me but also spurred me on to write the eulogy. Finishing my cup of tea, I thanked the family, briefly reading over my notes to ensure that I had everything I needed. The next time I would see them would be in the cathedral.

Leaving the Roussos family to their day, I am sure that they, like myself, reflected greatly on what we talked about that night. As I drove home, I threw ideas together in my head about what to include in the tribute and the best ways to write it. Over the coming days, I would need to become a little bit obsessed in order to do it justice. I would spend time on it in the evenings, as my time during the school day was focused on the children who were leaving, a more difficult task in this particular year as our Year 6 were deeply affected by what had happened.

The last day of term came and I believe it was a very emotional leavers' assembly, which had to be led by Janette in my absence, as my eldest son was also leaving primary school on that day. Family should always come first, so I sat nervously in his school hall on a tiny chair that was buckling under my weight, hoping the chair would survive long enough for me not to embarrass myself, or him for that matter. I drove over to Tarleton later in the morning to find the normal things you see with the Year 6 children on their final day: overexcitement, tears, and signed shirts. It felt very strange that they would be leaving us and moving on, especially after the last couple of months.

Another element of the last week was a request from the Roussos family for some of the staff team to create a short video clip about Saffie, and in particular a memory of her, to be played at the funeral. As one may imagine, this was incredibly difficult for those staff members to verbalise, and to be able to hold themselves together for long enough to make the recording without their emotions getting the better of them. Somehow, they found the strength to complete this task for the family, for Saffie, and to pay tribute to her. In addition, some of her best friends also made videos, with the support of their parents, to express their memories and feelings about their friend whom they were missing desperately. At this stage, these children were nine years old, talking into a parent's phone describing happy times with their murdered friend. This is an unthinkable situation for a child of that age to be in, but this was where they were and, like the adults, they wanted to do their best. What an impossible situation for both the children and their parents. They all did an incredible job for the family and for Saffie.

During that week we had needed to make preparations for the funeral and to communicate with staff and our community in doing so. This was in line with the family's wishes, and Andrew and Lisa had organised for a section of Manchester Cathedral to be reserved for the school party, which would include staff, parents, and pupils. To ensure everything ran smoothly on the day, they needed to know the number of people in our community who would be in attendance so that there was appropriate amount of seating allocated. A few days prior to the end of term, I sent the following letter to our parents:

Dear Parents,

I am writing to provide you with details of the arrangements for Saffie's funeral, as has been requested by her family.

The funeral will take place at Manchester Cathedral on Wednesday 26 July 2017, commencing at 1.45 p.m. I would advise that, should you wish to attend, you arrive in plenty of time, as it is anticipated that there will be a high number of people in attendance.

The family have asked that if you are attending the funeral, please do not wear black.

The family are also reserving an area at the cathedral for the families of TCP. Should you wish to sit with other families from the school, please return the slip below.

Yours sincerely
Chris Upton

The slips that I had included on the bottom of the letter were returned and processed by the school office and the details shared with the family. There was a real concern that the funeral would be so popular, with the general public wanting to celebrate Saffie's life, that there could be an issue with our community physically getting into Manchester Cathedral. To alleviate this issue, we wrote back to all those parents who had returned their slips and would be attending the funeral, issuing them with a pass, should they need it, to ensure they could come into the cathedral with ease. Could you imagine the further impact on a child, one of Saffie's friends, should they come all the way to Manchester to celebrate their friend's life, at what would probably have been their first funeral, only to be turned away?

I had taken time to consider the best approach to the funeral in terms of staff and children and had arrived at a position on this matter. I felt that, while parents may well want to bring children, it would need to be their responsibility to do so. This would allow the staff to sit together in the same area of the cathedral so that we could all be together. The main reason for this was to allow them to grieve. They had held it together for so long, and comforted the children, listening to and engaging in very difficult conversations; now was the time for them to focus on themselves. I was quite strict on this and reserved a specific area for school staff. This upset one local person, who found my decision not to allow them personally to sit with the staff 'sickening' and I received an email expressing their views. Someone who had never met Saffie and who currently did not have children in our school felt it was OK to complain that I hadn't met with them to discuss it, despite my inviting them to meet with me the previous day after school. Strangely, as you may imagine, I was extraordinarily busy, and responded via email. I hadn't meant to upset anybody or cause offence but, as I explained to them, they were welcome to join us in the Tarleton area, just not with the staff, as I wanted to be able to support my staff and allow them to grieve. I didn't respond to their follow-up email and the connotations it left. I am sure this person was grieving too, but it was unfair of them to put this on me or the school. Sometimes you just have to take these things on the chin.

On the last day of the summer term, another school year disappearing before our very eyes, I imagined school staff up and down the country starting to celebrate a long summer of family time and fun. This might be at their local pub or sitting with something cold in their hand in the back garden, chatting to friends while the smoke of a BBQ floated by on a light breeze. This time, I wasn't. Instead, I was completing the finishing touches to Saffie's eulogy and emailing a lady called Marcia Wall. I should really give Marcia her full title: Canon Marcia

Wall. She was the Canon of Manchester Cathedral. Andrew had provided her details, as I wanted to visit the cathedral prior to the funeral on the Wednesday. In my mind, this was vital in doing a good job for the Roussos family and, of course, Saffie. Marcia returned my email, and after a few exchanges we agreed on two o'clock on Tuesday, the day before the funeral. She gave me the specific instruction to come through the Dean's entrance and ring the bell. I looked forward to meeting her, with a little trepidation, and getting the layout of the cathedral in my head as well any other information I could glean from her, so that I was fully prepared.

In the days between the email exchange and meeting Marcia, Saffie's eulogy, her tribute, was practiced and polished. I hadn't shared it with anyone, not even my wife, Lucy. This was common practice for me and was the same in any presentation I would have made in a job interview or, in the past, a best man's speech. I have always believed firmly, some may say arrogantly, that when you start sharing these things, a margin of doubt can sink in. This will ultimately lead you to question yourself, leading to a worse performance or execution of the task. I didn't want to give it half an effort, especially not now. So, my words were my own and my words were private, until Wednesday.

Tuesday arrived, and the final part of my preparation was to travel to Manchester and visit Manchester Cathedral. Growing up in the 1980s, my father had instilled in me a phrase that would not perhaps be as acceptable now: Piss Poor Preparation = Piss Poor Performance. The trip to Manchester, therefore, was vitally important to me, and my attention to detail would ensure I did a good job for the family tomorrow. I would be catching the train to the funeral, so I took the train to Manchester on that Tuesday, leaving the car at home. My second-eldest son had spotted a free lunch, so travelled with me. As the train drew into Victoria Station, I couldn't help but think about the events of 22 May. The station forms part of the Arena, and it felt strange being there, where all of this had occurred and so many innocent lives were lost. You couldn't help but feel sadness coupled with the reality of a city that was still busy; the image of the Manchester bee personified.

Making our way through the station, the added security was noticeable. Although we were much earlier than we needed to be, to take into account a spot of lunch, we initially made our way through central Manchester and had a short walk to the cathedral, on a recce to get our bearings and look for the sign for the Dean's entrance that Canon Marcia had mentioned. It took a little while, but we found it tucked away around the back of the cathedral. We must have looked like burglars sizing up our next job. Lunchtime beckoned and, as my son and I were the only ones in our family who appreciated a little sushi, we made our way to the Arndale Centre and grabbed two stools at the Yo Sushi restaurant. It was nice to have that time with him. I had been so busy and so preoccupied with everything else that I knew I needed to really focus on my own family during the holidays, and we discussed our upcoming holiday to France, to visit my parents, that would begin in a couple of days.

We made our way back to the cathedral through the bustle of shoppers and workers enjoying their lunchbreak, finding Marcia, who greeted us warmly. She invited us into the offices at the rear of the cathedral and we sat down. She was lovely with my son, who seemed nervous and had gone quiet. She also made me at ease and went through the practicalities of the service. She asked about the eulogy that I would be giving and requested a copy. She was being prepared, just in case something untoward might happen and I was left in a position where I didn't have a copy to read from, perhaps due to leaving it on the train or it falling out of my pocket. I agreed to email it over to her later that day, which I did. She then took us into the cathedral itself. I wouldn't consider myself a terribly religious man, but have always had an interest in the architecture of churches and places of worship, as they can be quite spectacular. This was certainly the case as I stood in Manchester Cathedral. I was in awe of my surroundings; the attention to detail and that feeling of reverence engulfed me. The magnificent stained-glass windows streamed light into the vast, cavernous space. Marcia walked me around, showing me where the key areas would be: for example, where we would sit, where I would stand to deliver the tribute, and where the family would be. This really helped me to visualise what it would be like in around twenty-four hours' time. She then showed me a little wooden bee. Twenty-two bees had been created to symbolise the twenty-two victims of the attack. The bees also symbolised the spirit of Manchester, a spirit that would not be broken by such a pointless and cowardly act. Each bee would be blessed, and each victim's bee embossed into a piece of furniture in the cathedral as a point of remembrance. Marcia took us to a smaller area, containing red choir stalls, to show us where the bees would be placed. It was a kind, fitting tribute. I thanked Marcia for her time and, leaving the cathedral, we made the short walk back to Victoria Station and took the train home. It had been very worthwhile and had helped me to focus, putting myself mentally in the cathedral that evening, as I went over and over the words in the peace and quiet of my bedroom.

Chapter Eight

On the day of the funeral, I woke early with everything swirling around my head. It was pointless lying there, so I got up and looked over the words again. The paper was starting to get dog-eared and tatty, so I was pleased that I had printed more than one copy. A request of the family was that nobody should wear black, but that everyone should bring a flower – a rose. For practical reasons, I chose a buttonhole flower. I had arranged this at a florist local to where I lived a couple of days earlier and, on that morning, I took the opportunity to walk there, as this would help to gather my thoughts. Inside the florist, the lady chatted away to me, telling me how unusual it was to have a wedding on a Wednesday and asking me about it. I didn't have the heart to tell her where I was really going, as this would have made her uncomfortable, so I was very non-committal about it. While this seemed the best approach at the time, a few weeks later she came out of her house as I walked past to tell me that she had seen me on the news and just how terrible she felt for charging me, as she hadn't known who I was or where I was going on that day. I reassured her that it really wasn't an issue, and a pleasant conversation ensued. She happened to also be the Chair of Governors at a local academy and had been following the events, again thinking about what the impact could have been like for her school had they been in a similar position.

Over the last couple of months, I hadn't looked after myself particularly well. This would be something that I needed to address, as the first financial penalty of my self-neglect was the need to purchase a new suit for the occasion of Saffie's funeral; mine had become very snug. Showering and putting the suit on, I kissed Lucy goodbye. She was desperate to come with me and support me, but it was too soon to leave Arthur, who was still only a matter of weeks old. While it would be strange not having her with me, it was the right decision for the family and would ensure that I could focus on the staff and everything else going on that day. I made my way to Adlington train station and, when the Blackpool North to Manchester Airport arrived, it was full of familiar faces. We had organised ourselves well and different members of the team and governors had joined the train at various stops along the way, with a small handful of staff meeting us at Victoria Station. As we disembarked the train, I think many of us had similar feelings to those I had had the previous day. We quietly shuffled through the station, making our way over to the Printworks to find somewhere to eat, as we felt it would be best not only to all be together, but to try and eat something and look after each other's well-being on what was a poignant and difficult day.

Following lunch, we walked over to Manchester Cathedral. There was always going to be an interest in Saffie's funeral. She was the youngest victim and the last of the twenty-two to have their life celebrated, and therefore her funeral was symbolic to Manchester, a closing of a chilling chapter, maybe. It had captured people's imaginations. The press were out in force, positioned behind barriers which were there to control any possible crowds, so that those attending the funeral had the space to make it into the cathedral. Normally funerals are sombre, quiet affairs, but there was a real energy about what was going on outside the cathedral. Vibrant colours were everywhere, on people's clothes and in the flowers they either wore or carried. There were well-wishers lining the street by the cathedral and many others filed into the huge building. It was like nothing I had ever experienced. We joined the queue and made our way inside.

Finding the way to our area, we saw that members of our community were already seated. Children and parents were there, possibly not really knowing what to expect or what their reactions would be over the next hour. As the staff came in, this seemed to reassure the children; those familiar faces turning round and giving them that look as if to say, 'Everything is going to be OK.' They probably didn't even know they were doing it; it all came so naturally to them. All the children looked lovely and had dressed for the occasion in their Sunday best. It was such a shame that, at this stage in their young lives, they were about to say goodbye to their friend for the last time, something that would have deep ramifications for them in the months and years that would follow.

The cathedral continued to fill steadily over the next twenty-five minutes. On each seat, instead of an order of service, was a picture of Saffie, smiling up at everyone. When you turned it over you could read the words: 'We would like to thank you for being here today with us and for all your love and support.' Although they were quite a way away, opposite us sat the Chief Constable of Greater Manchester Police, Ian Hopkins, There was also the Mayor, Andy Burnham, whose profile had certainly been raised in the aftermath of the bombing, and who, in my opinion, had shown compassionate and strong leadership at a terrible time for his city. I know that he had been incredibly supportive to the Roussos family, and I imagine that would have been the same for the families of the other victims.

Like any funeral, we sat waiting, with quiet small talk occurring around the room. It was interesting, watching people, thinking about their link to Saffie and who they might be. Members of staff from Saffie's old school, Kew Woods, were there, and I chatted to the head teacher, whom I had known prior to the attack. It must have been so difficult for their staff, too. We sat waiting.

As music started to play, all heads turned to the entrance of the cathedral, as family members and close friends came into view. The song 'Faith' by Stevie Wonder featuring Ariana Grande filled the room as Saffie's little coffin entered. It was wicker and covered in many pink roses. It was really something to behold: a juxtaposition of beauty and the reality of what had occurred. Supporting the back of the coffin was Andrew, the weight of his daughter's body on his shoulder, close to her in the physical sense for one of the last times. It was horrendous to even contemplate. Behind them, Lisa walked with Xander, comforting him; her motherly instincts visible for all to see and her bandaged arm and slow limp further evidence of the attack. Her resilience in getting herself out of her wheelchair to walk into the cathedral that day was remarkable, and it was all for Saffie. Ashlee and other family members followed too, tears in their eyes and single pink roses in their hands. The beautiful coffin was placed in the centre of the cathedral, and the congregation looked on as the family took their seats at the front.

Sitting perpendicular to the family, my eyes were drawn to them, watching them. I am almost ashamed to admit it, but like so many others, we just wanted to be there for them. The service was underway and was presided over by the Reverend Rogers Govender, Dean of Manchester Cathedral. He welcomed the congregation inside the building, as well as those who had gathered outside to hear the service piped out to them through speakers attached to the stone walls of the cathedral. Very soon, a letter was read out to Saffie from her sister, Ashlee. It showed the love and warmth between the two sisters, something that wouldn't leave them with Saffie's death. Everyone just sat, listening, feeling devastated. Very soon, I was asked to come up to the lectern and give the eulogy for Saffie. Leaving my seat, everything went into slow motion. I could feel the eyes of my colleagues, parents, and children staring at me from behind. *What was he going to say? Was he going to be able to hold it together?* I arrived at the lectern, glancing up, as I shuffled my papers, to see a news camera at the back of the cathedral: something that until this point I had been unaware of. I felt a little bit more pressure from its presence. About two or three metres from me sat Saffie's family. To my right, again only a few metres away, lay Saffie, at rest. At this stage, you need to dig deep and find that little something that will make the difference and get you through. In the moment, I drew a deep breath and just focused on the family, telling the story of the life of a remarkable young lady. The words started to flow:

A very famous man by the name of Walt Disney once said, 'Laughter is timeless, imagination has no age, dreams are forever'. This is a good description of how Saffie lived her life, as nothing worried her, and she was determined to achieve what she wanted to achieve.

With her whole future in front of her, Saffie had many ambitions. Saffie dreamed big. She dreamed of being an actress or a singer, or both! In her schoolbooks she wrote about becoming as famous as her idol, Ariana Grande. Like many parents, you don't want to crush your children's dreams, just sprinkle a little reality on them. Lisa would tell Saffie that she needed a Plan B and would offer her suggestions. 'What about an Olympic gymnast?'

'No.'

'A teacher?'

'No.'

'What about this, what about that?' The answer always came back: 'No.'

She just wanted to be a star.

In school, her ambition was to be a member of the school council and this was something she achieved through dogged determination and an election campaign that would have given Donald Trump a run for his money. She masterminded the 'Vote Saffie' campaign, creating posters and sticker after sticker creatively by hand to ensure that her classmates made the right decision. She loved being on the school council and threw herself into planning events, and thoroughly enjoyed selling cakes for Macmillan and reindeer food at the Christmas Fair. All the time showing that quiet confidence that we saw so much and was such an endearing quality.

Even as a baby, Saffie enjoyed the attention. Living in Cyprus, she was the youngest child in her family and would be regularly passed around the adults.

Her first glimmer of celebrity came when she was only two years old. At the time she was living on the island of Kefalonia, and was at a Christmas party for the English community when she strutted her stuff on the dance floor for the first time. Being Saffie, she wasn't bothered that she was the only one dancing!

At this time, the family owned a clothes shop, where Andrew's beloved Harley-Davidson stood. Saffie, being as agile as she was, would regularly climb up onto the motorbike and sit on the fuel tank, causing Andrew to have a Basil Fawlty-like moment – crashing through the shop to get his daughter to safety. She, of course, just sat smiling.

Saffie's fearlessness features in many of her family's memories of her. Andrew bought her an electric chopper motorbike because she wanted a Harley-Davidson. He took her to the park to ease her into her new toy and, being the devoted dad, told her, 'If you're going to ride it, you need to listen to me.' Saffie knew better; Saffie was off into the distance while Andrew stood, his heart in his mouth, as his little girl flew round the park at twenty miles per hour, having the time of her life.

Andrew regularly worried about his little girl: it's what dads do. On her first sleepover with her friends Lily and Grace, it took all of Lisa's skills to stop Andrew going round in the middle of the night to bring her back home as he laid awake thinking about her, missing her.

She enjoyed going out with her sister, Ashlee. On one occasion they went to a trampoline park, where Saffie's daring side came out yet again as she climbed a ladder and backflipped six feet in the air into foam. While Saffie lay happily giggling, Ashlee stood shaking.

Saffie loved her family tremendously. She would sit in the chippy and make notes on the fish and chip paper for Lisa and Andrew, telling them both how much she loved them. These notes would be left subtly for Lisa on her pillow, or less subtly for Andrew, as he would be presented with them while in the middle of taking the chips out of the fryer.

Everything was a joke to Saffie, but on the rare occasion she upset someone, she would get upset too. At one time, Saffie had just got over a cold when Lisa got a dose of the norovirus. She was heartbroken as she thought she'd passed it on to her mum and made her unwell.

Saffie was headstrong and would never do anything that she didn't want to. She also realised how to get her own way: on a family holiday in Malta last year, her brother Xander returned to the family's meal table a little disappointed not to get a dessert, as there was an enormous queue. Saffie decided that this would not put her off. To everyone's surprise, she returned two minutes later with a dessert. That quiet confidence had kicked in and she had marched to the front of the queue and simply smiled at the people queuing, cheekily getting her own way.

While at Kew Woods School, she competed in the 'beanbag on the head' race at the annual Sports Day. She had to run with her other competitors to the end of the track, then turn round and come back. Halfway down the track her beanbag fell off. She was languishing in last place; however, she was down but not out. Saffie merely put the beanbag back on her head, turned, and ran back up the track, winning the race. Well, sort of winning the race.

I think it is fair to say that Saffie could get bored easily, unless it was her idea to do something. At the back of the chippy is a television screen, linked to a camera showing what is happening at the front. She would often go to the camera and perform dances, gymnastic routines, and backflips, knowing that she had a loving and admiring audience just feet away watching her on the TV screen. She'd also come into the shop smiling at customers. If they didn't pay her enough attention, she would do the splits or something of a gymnastic nature to ensure they were focused on her. Just outside the shop is a pole about fifteen feet tall. Saffie would climb to the top and cling on with one hand and swing. This resulted yet again in her poor father's heart being in his mouth while he would burst out of the shop to get her down! This was Saffie the joker at her finest.

Saffie had to be on the go at all times – when the family settled down for a movie, she wouldn't sit still and would do the splits in front of them. She also took great pleasure in winding up the family dog, Binky, as she was constantly picking her up and putting dresses on her. She even made Binky wear her Ariana Grande ears, and would hold her two front paws and dance with her around the living room. Saffie was only slightly more high maintenance than Binky, as she would change her outfits three or four times a day, and she really loved shoes. If Lisa or Ashlee left shoes lying around, and in particular high heels, she would put them on and dance round the house. Whenever she got any money, she wouldn't spend it on toys, but instead on clothes and shoes. Well, a superstar has to look their best!

When I think of Saffie, I cannot help but smile, thinking about getting to know her. Saffie and her classmates were all given the opportunity to learn a brass instrument. During the first lesson, I watched on with interest as different pupils were given their instruments. It came to Saffie's turn, and to my surprise she was given a trombone. The instrument looked huge next to her. Seeing the funny side, she had a little giggle - so too did her friends. Being too polite to say anything, she threw herself into playing it. It is fortunate really that Xander, her big brother, was so patient with her, as she would often be seen dragging the trombone case up the corridor at the end of the day, banging each wall on the way out while she gossiped happily with her friends. I often wondered how Andrew and Lisa fitted the trombone into their car, an Audi TT!

Saffie had a close bond with Xander, but would hide empty yoghurt pots in her brother's school shoes, so that when he put them on in the morning, she would get a reaction. The mischievous little sister didn't stop there: when Xander was out of the house, she would creep into his bedroom and play on his games – very often deleting things that he had saved!

Saffie was a great friend to everybody. She would laugh at her own mistakes, but would never laugh at anyone else's. She was a fantastic dancer, and during PE lessons she would help others in her group to perfect routines – she was a real team player. On her first day at our school her teacher buddied her up with another little girl to help her make friends. Saffie's excited new friend talked a lot that day. At one point, Saffie looked at her, smiled, put her finger on her lip and said, 'Shush!' Anyone else may have caused offence, but not Saffie - they became best friends.

It was a standing joke that she would always be slightly late for school. Most mornings, her teacher would ask the class if they had seen Saffie and would get the response, 'She'll be here in a minute.' A couple of minutes later, she would creep into the room, with that smile and those dimples, to a slight cheer from her friends. Saffie loved her family dearly. She was probably late due to the kisses and cuddles when saying goodbye to her mum and dad, and of course, the dog, Binky! Yet again her loving big brother would wait patiently for her. In an RE lesson about making sacrifices for Lent, she said that she would work in the family chippy to help everyone because everybody worked so hard. This makes me think of the wonderful clip shown on the news on Saffie's birthday, where she sings and dances in the kitchen while staff busily work behind her – she was clearly destined for great things.

Apart from her family, there was another love in her life. Ariana Grande. Saffie would come home from school and sit on the couch with her phone, playing all her songs, joining in word for word. Not content with keeping Ariana Grande to herself, she would make sure the staff from the chippy got involved, and got

81

them to sing and dance with her, creating lots of laughter – she was very persistent.

When Saffie found out that she had tickets to see her idol, she was counting down the days, and from Christmas she would excitedly talk about the concert and play videos on YouTube. Saffie was fiercely protective of Ariana and would regularly ask Ashlee who she liked best: Selena Gomez or Ariana Grande. Of course, like any big sister would, Ashlee would always choose Selena Gomez. Saffie just couldn't believe this! At one stage, in a discussion around celebrities, Lisa told Saffie that celebrities were Photoshopped – the notion that her Ariana Grande could be Photoshopped made her quite upset.

The irony of this tragedy is that the concert was a wonderful experience for Saffie – the happiest Lisa and Ashlee had ever seen her. Lisa rarely watched the stage that evening, but instead, her beautiful daughter, who knew every song, sang every word, and danced, I mean really danced, and didn't have a care in the world.

My final thoughts about Saffie are those of pride. Like everybody here, I am proud to have known this wonderful little girl whose outlook on life was and still is an inspiration to us all. So, as you leave the cathedral today, try to be more like Saffie: ambitious, good-humoured, loving, and compassionate. The world will truly be a better place.

Sleep tight, superstar.

With that I gave what was almost a court bow to the family, and turned to return to my seat. All the faces from the Tarleton Community area of the cathedral looked at me as I moved back towards them. At that point I couldn't take their faces in. The adrenaline was pumping round my body and I needed to sit and gather myself.

The funeral continued and Saffie's godmother, a talented singer from Cyprus, sang an acoustic version of 'Just the Way You Are' originally by Bruno Mars, with her partner providing the backing on a guitar. While it was beautiful to listen to, the congregation could clearly view her despair. The most moving part of the service was a tribute to his daughter by Andrew. It was raw and heartfelt. As a father myself, I just sat there, fully engaged, putting myself in his position. His love and anguish spilled out in equal measure. He spoke of such happy times, such happy relationships. You could not help but be moved by listening to him and watching him. One line that he said, that really moved me, was: 'I'm honoured to be her dad, honoured.' Knowing Andrew as I do now, this is still the case, and his obvious use of the present tense was as important then as it is now. During the service Andrew kissed Saffie's coffin, a sad, heartbreaking goodbye to his daughter.

There was a video montage shown with messages from friends and loved ones, many of which came from the school, the pre-recorded clips that staff and children had agonised over, finally given the light of day. The children's words, in particular, were deeply impactful in reflecting the loss of Saffie and the loss of their own childhood innocence.

Reverend Govender started to conclude the service, and in doing so brought forward one of the twenty-two wooden bees which would be embossed in the choir stalls. Asking Lisa to hold the bee, which she did, he gave it a blessing. This would live in the cathedral and honour Saffie's memory, as well as the other victims. The school had been asked if our choir would make a recording of 'Somewhere over the Rainbow' for the funeral. This was chosen by the family as the exit music. As the funeral party made their way out of the cathedral, the coffin again lifted by Andrew and other family members, our children's voices filled the air. Due to the amount of time that it took to get the congregation out of the building, it was played on a loop, and could still be heard playing when we got outside, as it sounded from the speakers.

Outside in the cathedral grounds, there were hundreds of people milling around, hugging each other and family members. I briefly hugged the family, who thanked me, then got out of their way. They had requested that the congregation leave the single roses that they had brought with them on the memorial cross that stands proudly to the right of the main entrance. Very soon, due to the huge amount of flowers, it was covered. It was a wonderful, bright, floral tribute to a wonderfully bright life lost. As a staff group, we stood chatting, speaking with parents who had attended as well as some of the children, comforting those who needed it.

The family returned to the funeral cars for a private cremation outside of the city. As they pulled away, spontaneous applause arose and rippled through the crowd, so that we were all clapping. It was probably a strange occurrence, but it felt quite natural. We were applauding and, in doing so, celebrating Saffie's young life. After a couple of minutes, the crowd began to disperse and move towards the city centre. It was only right that we found a local bar or pub to toast young Saffie's life. I was conscious that the press were out in force in the immediate area of the cathedral and, while they would probably in all likelihood have no interest in us, the last thing I wanted was for someone to take a picture of us doing just this, so I led the team a short walk away to a pub that was not only out of the way but could also accommodate us all. People had a drink and at different points left to catch various trains. By teatime there were four of us left, so we grabbed a bite to eat. I really needed this, and it was good to de-stress from the pressures of the day.

I left my remaining three colleagues to enjoy what Manchester had to offer. It was the summer holidays, and they deserved to let their hair down. The weather was appalling as I made my way through the wet, windy city. Manchester weather. As I moved through one of the squares towards the train station my phone rang. It was my friend Tony Currie, the head teacher of my neighbouring school. We probably should have been rivals, but we were both too interested in education and learning for all that nonsense, and instead worked together with other head teachers locally to do a good job for all the children in our rural area. At this stage, everything from the day and the preceding months was hitting me all at once. I was miserable and alone. Tony wouldn't have known, but that quick call to check in on me, telling me that he had been following the funeral and that I had done a good job, was what I needed at that exact moment in time. I will always appreciate him for that.

I needed to get home and see Lucy. Sitting on the train, I silently contemplated all that had happened that day, thinking about the Roussos family, the staff and how the children who were at the funeral were, as I am sure they would have struggled to settle at bedtime. As my train approached Bolton, an announcement came over the tannoy. Due to an incident, the train would terminate in Bolton. Someone had taken their own life further down the track. I called Lucy, who bundled Arthur into the car and came to get me. In the meantime, I waited in a rather rough pub by the station, the only man in there in a suit and, of course, a pink tie.

Chapter Nine

For all of our community, the long summer holidays were important in the healing process. That time was to re-engage with our families, to hide from the stresses of the last two months, particularly so for our children. I myself had escaped the day after the funeral, with my parents and young family, to a cottage in a very remote part of France on the Franco-Belgian border. It was incredibly quiet, but just what I needed – swimming in lakes with my older two boys and quiet walks past cattle in the early evening, while watching birds of prey hovering in the light blue sky. The evenings spent with my mother, enjoying a glass of wine while chatting about years gone by, or stargazing with my eldest son, were just what I needed to re-engage with them all. I recognised the strain the pressure was putting on me not too long after the Manchester Arena attack when, on a family walk, I had had a complete meltdown at one of my children. We had only just left the house and something was said, which ended, I am ashamed to admit, in an angry outburst by myself. I had stomped home, removing myself to our bedroom to lie on the bed and calm myself, gathering my thoughts. This was uncharacteristic of me, but was a sign that I needed to manage the pressure better. Although, on the surface, colleagues and our community probably thought I was doing well – which I was, but there was no hiding from the fact that I was mentally exhausted from it all. We all were, and I know that some members of staff were also experiencing similar situations. The trigger for me on this occasion was the terror attack at Borough Market in London. My dad was there twenty-four hours before it happened, going there on my recommendation. I felt awful, although he wasn't even in the country when it occurred, but my irrational brain had taken over.

Then, September, and the return to school was actually quite uneventful. It was really like the start of most academic years and, although we had had deep discussions, especially as a senior leadership team, we were quite surprised by it all. The children seemed happy to return to school and to be with us. Maybe this was because we made them feel safe, a safe place to discuss their worries. We went with this and tried to restore as much normality as we could, as this would support our children the best. This seemed to be the most logical thing to do.

One issue that had been playing on my mind was that of supervision for the staff. Supervision is well-used in many sectors, especially in health and mental health, as a means of supporting staff to focus on issues that may impede their performance at work, but also to promote positive well-being and mental health. It needs to be driven by the individual, with a supportive supervisor to acknowledge difficulties and use techniques to enable them to reach solutions, if they are possible. Supervision in education, particularly at this time, wasn't very popular. I had chatted long and hard with my brother-in-law about it, as he used it regularly as a mental health practitioner, and really shouted very loudly about the benefits it not only brought to himself, but also his staff. I was at the stage where, as a head teacher, I had been forced to be reactive to everything that had occurred, and I wanted to be more in control of what we were doing. I wanted to ensure that, as a leader, I had effective support for my staff at all times: to not learn from the lessons of the summer would be a huge missed opportunity. Disappointingly, I had first tried to access supervision via the Critical Incident Support Team in early June, but they never responded to my email. I took this as a sign and decided to source it elsewhere.

The first time I met Sally and Annie, from an organisation called Listening Tree, was on a course I had booked for myself and my colleague Lisa in Burnley, in the far east of Lancashire. The course itself gave us the basic skills to go away and implement in our school. At first, I was sceptical. For some reason, this happens very often with groups of head teachers. We have been working in an education system for so long that is at times relentless and unforgiving, from the various pressures that cascade down from central government, that we forget about ourselves. Some head teachers forget about their staff, too. Having done various exercises, I wasn't really getting it, so I asked Annie, 'But what actually is it?' Annie explained what it was, but I think it means different things to different people and I needed to see it in action.

We arrived on the second day of training the following day, and this time Annie was joined by Sally. I liked Sally instantly. She was what I call a 'proper Northerner', with a gruff voice that was caring and compassionate while also making you smile. As a former nurse in a hospice, she had a lot of experience of bereavement. She led a group supervision session and I just got it. I could now see how it might work in our school, so that our staff were looked after and we had the opportunity to put their well-being at the forefront of what we did, as this would have positive outcomes both for the adults and the children in our school. Lisa and I busily, almost excitedly, discussed our ideas and plans as part of a breakout session. By the end of the second day, we were able to take the notion of supervision back to school, and we began to timetable training and systems so that it was both cost-effective and focused. We created an effective system that we still use to this day, which allows the staff the time to reflect and be supported. I didn't realise at this stage just how important supervision would be, in the months ahead, to support us all and give us that little space to breathe. One of the most gratifying parts of leading my team was the reality that, despite all the tough moments and hard days, not one member had a day off, which is truly an achievement.

I was proud of the work we were doing in the area and that we were flying the flag for staff well-being. In the months and years that followed, we were successful in developing our systems to encapsulate all staff who wanted it, as well as sharing good practice with other schools in leading staff training or meeting with other senior leaders in different schools. We shared our resources so that they could consider and develop a bespoke model for their school, as a one-size-fits-all system certainly is not appropriate. I think it is sad that many schools have struggled to incorporate approaches like supervision into their practice, as if and when something goes wrong, they would have something in their toolkit that would make the difference.

A real positive from the supervision training was the link we had made with Listening Tree, as a strong relationship developed between our organisation and theirs. Over the next few years, they would be by our side supporting us and our children, sometimes dropping everything to help us when I called them.

They found funding streams to help us with therapeutic support for our children and really just went out of their way to be there for us. They have been our guardian angels.

As the autumn term progressed, children started to struggle emotionally. Many were Saffie's closest friends. Like anyone who is grieving, things that they had done together with Saffie stuck in their minds, causing them upset. The advice we had previously been given in the initial aftermath was that we needed to allow the children to grieve and that this was normal. If we intervened too early, this could damage their development and coping mechanisms moving forward. While I respected this advice, we all found it incredibly difficult, as we all wanted to wave a magic wand and make it better. Colin, the counsellor who had contacted us in the initial aftermath, was working in school, and so too was our new learning mentor. The work was very much on bereavement and supporting the children to try and make sense of it all.

Parents were starting to struggle with their children at home too, particularly around bedtime. You see, the children were scared. Looking back to 2017, it was a year of terror. It was all over the news. In March, there was the Westminster attack, where a terrorist drove a car which killed four pedestrians, then stabbed a police officer; in May, the Manchester Arena attack; in early June, the London Bridge attack, where a van ploughed into pedestrians before the terrorists inside ran to Borough Market, stabbing innocent civilians with long knives. But there was still more to come in this truly terrible year. Later in June, we had the Finsbury Park attack, with one person killed and many others injured when a van was driven into a group of innocent worshippers outside a mosque; then in September, the Parsons Green attack, where an improvised explosive device was detonated on a busy tube train, injuring twenty-two people. Outside the UK, there were attacks all round the world, including in Europe. For example, there was the Barcelona attack in August. Imagine being a child who had lost their friend in a terror attack, already scared. The attacks kept happening and happening and happening. A parent couldn't simply tuck them up in bed, kiss them on the head and tell them that it was a one-off and that everything would be OK. It had become a very difficult situation to deal with.

We went on supporting the children, and were fast approaching the six-month anniversary of the attack when something unusual occurred that gave me an insight into planning support and approaches moving forward, especially when we came to consider what we would do around the first anniversary of the Manchester Arena attack. I received an email from Louisa, a publicity and events executive at HarperCollins Publishers. David Walliams had written a new book called *Bad Dad*, and was promoting it in a live event at the Palace Theatre in Manchester. Following on from his visit earlier on in the year, they had gifted the school twenty tickets to give to our choice of children in any way we deemed fit. We wrote to parents, as it was only a couple of days away, and we needed to be sure that they would be able to take them to Manchester at the weekend so that tickets were not wasted. During an assembly we pulled names out of a hat. This was exciting for the children, and really lifted the mood momentarily.

The children who went to the event reported back that they had had a wonderful experience seeing David on the stage again. I reflected on the effect it had had on the children. It was almost certainly unplanned, but the layering up of support and concern from David Walliams and HarperCollins was impactful. Not only had David visited the school and generously donated his time and books, but months later, he was still being kind and thinking about them. Kindness is often underestimated, but in showing it, our children felt loved. Whatever we did in the coming months ahead, we would need to have a targeted approach, layering it so that we built on what we had done previously; this would support our recovery. Another important factor was that it needed to be fun – these were children, after all.

Days later came the six-month anniversary of Saffie's death. It isn't usual that this short amount of time is reflected upon, but it must have been a slow news day, as quite a lot of coverage was given. I made a decision to address this in a singing assembly, and we sang two songs. The first was a revisit to May and Journey's 'Don't Stop Believing'. This was followed by Katy Perry's 'Roar', a song that we would come to sing many times, almost as a battle cry to say that we would be strong. The children really struggled through this. There were many tears and staff intervened to support them in a sight that had become ever so familiar: children hugging and comforting one another. It appeared to mark the start of a new chapter in the grief process for some of the children.

As the months continued to progress towards the first anniversary, we certainly saw that some of our children's grief, their open distress, was growing. Colin continued to work with the children we had identified, counselling them on an individual basis. Our new learning mentor had a better-paid job offer, so left us in the December, leaving Janette and I to pick up some of the work for half a term. This was incredibly difficult at this point in the process. We had fortunately been able to recruit a new, highly skilled learning mentor called Tracy Wren to start at the end of February, bringing with her a wealth of experience. This was such an important appointment for us, and her work over the coming years would be vital in supporting our children. At her interview, we had made it clear how important the role was and the obvious reasons why, but I don't believe she truly knew what she was walking into. She just didn't sense it.

On her first day, Janette introduced Tracy to some of the children most affected, and she started to build a relationship with them, a relationship that would be vital over the next year-and-a-half of their young lives as they grew to depend on her. I once asked Tracy what it was like when she first came into the school and joined our team. Her response was that she was dumbfounded by what we had provided for the children and the compassion and support we had given. She was also blown away with the raw emotion in the school, especially when she had to broach the subject of Saffie. Tracy, like the professionals who supported us, would come to lead so many difficult discussions in our road to recovery.

It was at a similar time that I was first made aware of the Manchester Resilience Hub through a governor who had links within that particular field of expertise, and who put us in touch with them to see what support they might be able to offer us. I met a lead clinical psychologist from the hub a few weeks later, in my office, with another one of her colleagues. She was quirky, kind, and incredibly intelligent. I instantly liked her and felt free to open up and share where we were as a school. She seemed surprised that we hadn't heard of the Resilience Hub, and that nobody had signposted us to them – a further example of the issues the complexities of North West politics and its various council structures had played in slowing support for those affected by the attack. Our council had certainly not shared the information.

One of the key discussion points with her was around the support for the first anniversary of the Arena attack. We focused on different ideas, what to expect, and what support might be needed. We took a lot of leaflets to share with our families so that they themselves could make contact, should they need to, and a number of them did at various stages. One thing I tried to do at one stage was to get the hub to run some form of face-to-face support locally. I believed that this was important across the two villages of Tarleton and Hesketh Bank, due to having two of the victims of the attack so closely associated with them. While this never came to fruition, the hub appeared to do more work on a phone call basis, as this was their remit. They were dealing with such a high number of affected individuals, most of them young people.

Within our school, some of the children were starting to think deeply about how Saffie had died and many difficult questions were asked of staff and the counsellors. They also had their own thoughts about the manner in which she had died, which were shattering to listen to. Some had thoughts of a cartoon bomb, a fuse lit like in an old Tom and Jerry movie, while others depicted more realistic imagery. Can you imagine being that adult? Finding the right words at such a delicate time? For a large group of children, you could visibly see how worn out they were with their grief. Their tiredness, their despair. While some had been diagnosed with PTSD, you could see that others had similar symptoms. At times some of them looked like lost souls, their eyes empty, staring. At other times they would be openly crying, not able to deal with simple day-to-day tasks. We struggled to keep them in class, learning, and needed to put provision in place for them to leave lessons if they were not coping. As our learning mentor, Tracy would pick up these children in an attempt to support them and get them emotionally in a place where they could go back into a classroom. Some became heavily reliant on Tracy, needing constant reassurance to get through a day – their mental health and well-being was our top priority, but we were also concerned about the huge chunks of learning they were missing and the impact this could have throughout their education and life.

This was such a challenge for staff. I wanted them to create as much normality as possible while also being ready to support the children at the drop of a hat. The teachers and teaching assistants did well at this, and I would often see a child in tears being comforted by an adult in class or just outside the classroom while the learning continued: perhaps a metaphor for life. The thing is, I knew how devastating it was for the children. It was a hugely adverse childhood experience, but I was desperate to ensure that it wouldn't rob them of their childhood and, equally, their education. So, when they were having better days, it was important that they learned that through the tough months ahead around the first anniversary, it was OK to celebrate Saffie's life and at times have fun doing so – this was important to the children. Their time with Saffie had been spent having such fun – it was important to her memory that we put this in the forefront of our minds.

Chapter Ten

The build-up to and planning of the first anniversary was a complicated and difficult task, in the most part because of the pressure I put on myself to get it right. It was clear that, to make a good job of it, I would have to liaise regularly with Andrew and Lisa.

We were fortunate that we still had a lot of money in Saffie's fund, which had been gifted to us from various individuals, schools, and other organisations. This really made the difference at this time, because it gave us options in our approaches and allowed us to access the best and, at times, most innovative ways to commemorate and celebrate Saffie's life while supporting the well-being of our children and staff.

My first idea came to me as I was driving to work one day. Saffie was a little star in the making and her family felt deeply about this, wanting her to remain in people's minds for being the cheeky entertainer she was, making people smile. I had been to London many times and enjoyed spotting the English Heritage blue plaques on various buildings to denote whether somebody famous had lived there, was born there, or had done something else remarkable there. They came into existence in 1866 and were a much-respected way of honouring chosen people – perfect for Saffie. I began researching the background and further information relating to the blue plaques and was able to get in contact with London Plaques, who made them for English Heritage. Susan Ashworth, their director, was most helpful and, although it was a tight turnaround for May, due to the slow drying of the ceramic prior to firing, she felt that if we got the information to her quickly, it was doable. I made contact with the family, who loved the idea. We liaised with them, as well as Saffie's friends, to come up with three words to describe her and to go on the plaque, so that the final design we sent to Susan read:
SAFFIE-ROSE ROUSSOS
2008–2017
Beautiful, Captivating and Kind
learned here

2015–2017

Susan was really taken with the project and provided a first-class service to us, taking photographs of the plaque in its various stages, including when it was initially cast and when the letters were first put onto it. It was wonderful to see it taking shape. We had made the decision that we wanted the plaque high up at the back of the building so that it was overlooking the playground. To me, that seemed the natural place for it to be – a place where Saffie and her friends had played so happily. The only criticism I had about this decision was one I heard third-hand from one of my teachers. An elderly gentleman had been walking down a public path at the side of the school, looking for the plaque months later, and was upset that it couldn't been seen by the public.

We also created a stage that would be situated just below the plaque. Saffie loved to dance, so we wanted to encapsulate her personality on the playground. Sharing the ideas with her family, we came up with 'The Saffie-Rose Roussos Theatre', which name was displayed on the backdrop with a single rose. This area could be enjoyed by so many other children and would be a lovely reminder of Saffie's life with us all.

I knew that the family would be in the region around the time of the anniversary as they were now living many miles away. We wanted to hold a short gathering to acknowledge the anniversary and to celebrate Saffie's life. We therefore started to plan and organise what we called a Celebration of Life, for 21 May, a day prior to the first anniversary due to the family's plans on the day itself.

This would be the first time that the family had been back to the school since that fateful night and we, as a staff, felt nervous. We wanted to make them feel welcome and to do them proud in what we had organised. This was a time of real grief, so much so that a couple of weeks prior to the planned event, I had organised for colleagues from the Resilience Hub to come to school to do two sessions, firstly for the staff and secondly for some of the parents. We were all struggling to support the children. The impending anniversary was a real trigger for them, with their mental health visibly worsening and the absences from class and so from learning increasing rapidly. The rawness in the school was unbelievable, and we all felt it every day. It was clear from some of the children that they had a fear about the date itself.

At a similar time, I had been approached by the BBC to record our choir singing, for a special programme as part of our regional news broadcast, *BBC North West Tonight*. They would combine four choirs from different educational institutions that had suffered a loss at the Arena. The chosen song was 'Somewhere over the Rainbow', something familiar, as we had recorded it for Saffie's funeral. The presenter, Annabel Tiffin, came to the school as part of the recording. The children did a fantastic job, as they always did, singing beautifully, but were all very emotional. Annabel and I talked about it and she was clearly moved by what she was seeing. She made a comment that obviously the song was having an impact on them. She was right for some of the children, but I pointed out to her that for a proportion of the children, this was currently very normal and was just what the school was facing at that time. Seeing someone external feel what we were feeling was interesting, and it was clear to see both the shock and sadness on her face. Like us, she just wanted to make it all go away for the children.

As we moved into May, one of Saffie's closest friends made the comment, 'It's May.' When pressed they explained that they had been dreading it becoming May due to the anniversary and the upset they would feel. I think that this reflection, from a primary school-aged child, is important to note. Trauma can be based on a perception of the future in combination with the events of the past.

The two sessions with the Resilience Hub were upon us, and I attended both. Firstly, we met as a staff team. All of the teachers were there, and many other staff volunteered to attend too. The lead psychologist was incredibly supportive, but such a bespoke session was new to her and her colleagues too. Supporting a large group of staff who were feeling as tired and low as we all were almost a year after a terror attack was fairly unique. As the psychologists in the room facilitated the session, there was an outpouring of grief. I found it incredibly difficult to sit and listen to my colleagues share their thoughts, the pressures, the difficult conversations with the children. There were tears, a lot of tears. It was all so tense. Numbing. I still get a lump in my throat when

96

I think of it. It took me right back to when we first found out that Saffie had died; it felt the same and, at this point, time had not healed the wounds that had been exposed for so long. We may have concealed them, but they were there. The session was obviously needed and, looking back on it some years later, I realise that it allowed us to get our feelings on the table and supported us all as a team, forming part of our recovery process.

I didn't think that the second session with the parents could be any worse, but I was wrong. It was equally as stomach-churning as the first, but here we had a group of mothers wanting to do their best for their children, and they were worried and scared. What we were seeing at school was being replicated at home and those children were uncontrollably hurting. We did a task where we wrote down questions or feelings on a Post-it note, and these were displayed on a large board at the front of the room to draw reference to. In the middle of the brightly coloured array of paper was a question written by one of our mums that gave meaning to everything we had done as a school and would continue to do on our journey of recovery. The Post-it note read: 'When will I see the sparkle in my little girl's eyes again?' It was such a gut-wrenching but poignant question and I knew in an instance that, in what we had done – the counselling, the therapy, the fun events like David Walliams' visit, and what we would continue to do and plan – we were searching for the sparkle.

I drove home that evening in silence. Emotionally, I felt like I had been hit by a train. Everything swirled endlessly in my head, and I tried to consider if there was ever a time when I had felt so incredibly low. It was all so relentless, and, at the time, there was no sign of it ending. I just wanted a magic wand to make it all better. This clearly wasn't an option; we would all have to keep pulling together.

Another issue, a week or so prior to the anniversary, was that of the statutory tests for our Year 6 children, which are called SATs. For some reason, the Friday before testing week, we had a serious issue with our Year 6 classes. They had been talking on the playground about their SATs and a couple had expressed concerns that a terrorist may come into the room where they were taking their tests and detonate a bomb. The very mention of this spread like wildfire amongst the children, and all of a sudden, while other schools up and down the country were quietly completing last-minute preparations, we were working with our children to provide them with reassurance and support so that they would at least walk into the room the following week. It seemed so unfair that we would be judged the same as all the other schools that year, so following the tests, I applied for compensatory marks for them all and was successful in my application. This was the only way that I could ensure some realm of fairness for those children.

As the Celebration of Life came ever closer, I started to get some interest from the press and received telephone calls and emails to see what we were doing to mark the anniversary and whether or not they could be part of it. On the whole these were the professional media outlets, Sky News being one of them. But after the previous year, this wasn't about the press; it was about our school community coming together privately and the Roussos family being able to come to our school out of the way of the cameras. I had also been approached by a BAFTA award-winning documentary team that had asked to film in the school as part of a landmark three-part documentary looking at how the threat of terrorism was affecting the world that we live in. They had produced critically acclaimed documentaries such as *The Murder Detectives* and *Damilola, Our Loved Boy*. But there was no way that I could allow them to film in our school at this time; the effect on the children and staff would have been catastrophic. I politely declined their offer; in fact, I politely declined all offers, in order to safeguard us all.

A further concern for the Celebration of Life was press intrusion. While I could stop the press from coming onto the school property, there was little I could do to stop them coming down a public footpath and taking photos of the event. I had thought long and hard about this, wanting to ensure that this didn't occur and upset Saffie's family or friends. So, I hatched a plan. I am fortunate to have so many supportive families and parents at my school. I picked up the phone and called one of them, who just happened to own their own logistics firm. I explained that I had a strange request and shared what was in my mind: a cunning plan. There was laughter at the other end of the phone before they confirmed that they would support me fully.

Therefore, on the day, they drove a couple of lorries with long trailers to school and parked them in a line to obscure the view onto the playground from the public footpath. We then got some material to block out underneath the trailers, creating a total screen. While we received many strange looks as guests arrived that afternoon, it did its job well. After all the effort we had gone to, of course, no-one-from the press turned up, not even one. But at least we were prepared, and it reflected the lengths our community would go to support us and Saffie's family.

A further issue was getting support from the police for the events that we would be holding around the first anniversary. This was a time when the police were on their knees after years of budget cuts, resulting in issues with the basic number of boots on the ground. I had tried making contact with the Rural Policing Team, based in the town of Ormskirk, on countless occasions but had had no response to my many emails and answerphone messages. Thinking around the problem, I spoke with one of my parents, who was an officer for Lancashire Constabulary. He was able to quickly put me in contact with the right person and I organised for their support, which made me feel better – we wanted to leave no stone unturned in making a success of what we were doing.

It was all a very stressful time. One of the main issues in the days before the event came from the arrival, or should I say lack of arrival, of the blue plaque. We were already concerned that it simply wouldn't be made on time, as an element in the manufacturer's kiln had stopped working and had taken a number of days to repair. They had kindly prioritised our plaque to get it finished and, with only a matter of days to go, Susan had let me know that it was being couriered to Tarleton from her home in Cornwall. The problem was, it never arrived. By this stage it was Friday evening and the event was on Monday. Using the tracking number, I located it three hundred miles from Tarleton - in Plymouth. It appeared the courier had misread the postcode. I managed to liaise with the courier firm as calmly as I could and soon it was on its way up north. All that went on in my mind was: would it make it in time? I am pleased to say that it did, and on the morning of the Celebration of Life, I picked it up from the depot and got it to school. It looked wonderful, and the single dark pink rose that had been added to it was perfect. The next problem was fixing it to the wall, as it was incredibly heavy and I hadn't given this enough consideration. Fortunately, one of our local tradesmen quickly came to the site and solved the problem for us, creating a metal frame for it to be secured to the wall, not charging us a penny.

The event was imminent, and I had previously arranged for Andrew and Lisa to come slightly early, as it would be an emotional and difficult return for them, coming back to the school. This would help them get their bearings around how the event would work prior to our community joining us. I heard the car pull up in the car park and walked out of my office to the main entrance of the school, where I stood and greeted them. It was visibly difficult for them, especially for Lisa, who was just so upset that I wondered if she would actually come into the school at all. She is such a remarkable person and, with some kind, supportive words, we managed to get her into the school and to a quiet room and cup of tea to settle her. Xander was there too, and it was lovely to see the young man that he was growing into. I was delighted that he would be the family member to unveil the plaque, and he had also prepared a short speech.

The event was well supported by our community, including parents, carers and grandparents, as well as representatives from schools in our local education community, and, of course, our school adviser. I welcomed everybody briefly before handing over to our school choir, who performed a song called 'Rise Up', that had been written by one of our talented teachers. This was followed by the reading of a poem called 'Superstar', read by another teacher. I had searched long and hard for a poem for the event but couldn't find anything that was appropriate, so I wrote one myself, encapsulating the three words that described Saffie on the plaque, signing it as Anon. The poem read:

Superstar, shining bright,
You filled our lives with love and light,
We think of you every single day,
The fun, the laughter and the play.

Your smile, those eyes,
Always ready to surprise,

Now immortally from afar,
The world's most courageous little star.

Here your friendship grew and grew,
Through tears, we remember you,
We wish for a world at peace,
Where bitterness and hatred cease.

We knew your life to be,
With friends and family,
Happy, loving, caring,
Adventurous and daring.

At the forefront of our mind:
Beautiful, Captivating and Kind

Xander unveiled the plaque, which was given a nod of approval by the large crowd that had gathered. It was a fitting tribute. This was followed by a minute of applause in memory of his younger sister, before Xander made a short speech of thanks. It was quite something, seeing him stand up there so confidently. Adolescence was changing him, and I was so proud of him and the manner in which he was conducting himself, and the way he appeared to take it all in his stride. The choir finished the celebration, singing the Oasis hit 'Don't Look Back in Anger', an anthem of solidarity following the Manchester Arena attack. The lovely part of the event was the milling about afterwards. We had sent an SOS out to our parents for cakes, which we had set up in the hall in order to have tea and cake together – it was a celebration, after all. Our community didn't let us down, and there were so many donations, with everyone wanting to do their bit on such a special occasion. I chatted with Andrew and Lisa, and it was lovely to see them reconnect with other parents on the playground. The event had been a success. As the community and the Roussos family left the school site, while we breathed a sigh of relief that it had gone so well, our attention turned to tomorrow and the children, for the real first anniversary.

Many of the children were anxious about the day and, as we had had a more formal event the evening before with the family and our community, I decided that the day should be focused on the children and should become a celebration of childhood innocence, something that had been so viciously attacked in the last year. We were about to take lemons and make lemonade, giving the children a day not only to remember to but to make their eyes sparkle again. This was again made possible by the fund we had accrued through the generosity of the public, schools, and other organisations over the past year. Looking back, it was an incredibly important way to spend a small proportion of that money.

The children arrived at school in their own clothes that morning, ready to be put into smaller groups, with a carousel of activities planned over a variety of areas, which would give them a fun day of celebration. The staff all made suggestions about the activities they wanted to offer, based on their own interests or something that they thought would appeal to the children. We had timed slots for each activity and rotated them across the morning. I based myself on the playground and had set up a game called Danish Long Ball, which was similar to rounders and was something that, once taught, the children loved. It was fantastic to hear them laughing and having fun. Elsewhere around the school we had various craft activities occurring, making mood jars, pond dipping, and yoga in the hall to name but a few. There was even a mobile farm in our Early Years outdoor area. The children were simply having an amazing time, and we reinforced that this was OK, because it was.

It was always potentially going to be a difficult day for the staff, so we provided some food at lunchtime to ensure that they had eaten well and were being looked after. A custom, which had developed at Easter, was that the Roussos family would kindly bring fish and chips to the school at lunchtime on the last day of term as a gift to all the staff. I have to say, they were delicious, and we kept this in mind when planning the day, as it was fitting that we replicated this event with fish and chips from a local chippy. The sentiment and the stodge were much needed, in equal measure.

We were also prepared to offer emotional support to the children, with a range of professionals joining us, just in case. Colin was there, alongside Sally and Annie from Listening Tree, as well as Asa, a new governor and parent with professional expertise in this field. We didn't need direct support for our children on that particular day; however, I reflected that it was good to have those professionals with us. They had become part of our family in such a short space of time and it was only right that they were there.

The highlight of the week was the second visit of the Roussos family in two days. As a family, it must have been hugely challenging, considering how to mark the first anniversary of their daughter's death. There were church services occurring in Manchester itself, the main one being held at Manchester Cathedral and attended by Duke of Cambridge and the Prime Minister. These were an option, but knowing Andrew and Lisa as I do now, that wouldn't have been their style. A few days before the anniversary, Andrew called me with an idea that could only be considered in equal parts both madcap and wonderful. He wanted to get a group of bikers together to ride from Preston to Manchester, stopping off at key points on the way, including our school in Tarleton and the chippy in Leyland. I loved the idea, but Andrew was concerned that at such late notice there wouldn't be lots of them. We started making arrangements and agreed to speak the next day. The thought of there not being many bikes turning up played on my mind that evening and I sat racking my brain for a solution. I certainly wasn't a biker. Growing up on the island of Jersey, it was a rite of passage for any sixteen-year-old to get a 50cc motorbike to potter round the island on. I was no different, but at times it had had disastrous consequences for me, as I was totally useless on mine, hitting the ground on numerous occasions. There was also one incident where I got a little overexcited coming around a countryside corner, leaving the bike in a field and me in a tree. I was certainly safer in a car. Having given the issue of finding bikers much thought, I had an idea. As a Freemason, I was aware of a group of bikers within our organisation called the Widows Sons. They got together regularly to enthuse about their love of all things on two wheels and held ride outs to raise money for charity. Fortunately, there were quite a few in my Masonic lodge. I made contact with one of them and that attracted a few riders. This would support the family, but I believe the Harley-Davidson

103

riders were a little concerned, as they were quite selective about who they rode with, particularly for health and safety reasons. I can't say that I blamed them. Andrew, too, had managed to recruit a few more. It was happening, and I purposely kept things under the radar as I was never sure how legal it all was, so thought it best to keep quiet and feign ignorance if anybody asked.

At lunchtime, all the staff and children assembled in the front car park of the school, ready for the bikers and Roussos family. We had all moved our cars so that they could come into the car park for a moment's reflection. We positioned the children in a safe area, just in time to hear the noise of a large group of motorbikes that grew louder and louder, until we could set eyes on them. They began flooding into the gate: there must have been thirty of them all there, the children waving them in, led by Andrew on his Harley-Davidson. Lisa, Ashlee, and Xander were there too, pillion passengers who only made us aware that it was them when they peeled their helmets off. Everyone parked up, getting carefully off their bikes, and stood around chatting. I noticed a commotion at the far side of the car park from the children, with a group of them excitedly saying, 'Look, it's Chesney!' Looking at the slim, red-headed biker, I could see that they were right, and that, in the space of a year, the second-most famous Chesney had now visited Tarleton. This time it was Sam Aston, the actor who plays Chesney Brown in the long-running soap *Coronation Street*. He was humble and had given his time to support the family, and was more than willing to have his picture taken with some of our children. Xander, too, joined in at this point.

I led a minute's silence, which was an important part of the day: that quiet reflectiveness that had led us all to this point, standing in our car park with all these people and motorbikes. It must have looked a strange sight to the farmers bobbing past on their tractors or people walking their dogs. Andrew and I shook hands before I hugged Lisa goodbye. The experience was hugely impactful on everybody there. What I loved most about it was that they had done it their way, on their terms, and taken charge of a horrible situation. This had helped our children enormously. The engines roared again and, as the deafening sound eventually disappeared, it was time for ice cream and back to celebrating the innocence of childhood. What should have been a terribly challenging day, wasn't. We had all pulled together to ensure the children were loved and supported. We knew we had achieved it: the momentary sparkle in their eyes told us so.

Chapter Eleven

As the summer term drew on, we continued to focus on supporting the children who needed it most. By now, this was a smaller group, although from time to time we would need to support others. I wanted to focus on the work we had already done to support our children and promote positive mental health and well-being, giving the school and children a couple of projects.

The first opportunity for doing so presented itself as part of an art-based initiative called Bee in the City. Organisations could purchase giant bee sculptures that would be painted and decorated, before being returned to the organisers with a brief description of the bee. These were all to be displayed in public buildings or outside locations around Manchester. For me, this was perfect. It would allow a small group of children to develop something special that had a link to Manchester, and would eventually give us a reason to get them into the city, reducing any fear they may have while under the watchful eye of our supportive and skilled staff. This could really help them to move on.

Another aspect of the bee was that it would also allow us to involve our two neighbouring schools. We invited a small group from each after the design and concept was completed and we were ready to decorate the bee, or, as we called it, The Little Superstar. It probably would have been easier just to do it ourselves, but I also wanted the project to acknowledge the support of our local education community over the last year, as well as to acknowledge that it wasn't just our school that had been affected. Many children from all schools, irrespective of the colour of their jumper or type of logo they wore, would have been frightened in the aftermath of the attack. The combination of the pink and yellow ribbons throughout the villages showed solidarity, but at the same time reminded them of those events daily. I wanted them to be involved, too. I'm not sure how our own children felt about this, as they were incredibly protective of the bee. But it was good to have children from different schools working on the project, and it was a coming together of young minds in such a positive manner. Enjoying the arts and being creative is a cornerstone of any childhood, and all the children involved appeared to have thoroughly enjoyed themselves, although I am sure the drinks and biscuits played their part as well.

The production of the bee was in full swing over the period of the first anniversary, so it was fantastic to show the Roussos family how it was coming together when they visited the school. What was lovely was that as well as the children from different schools adding their brush strokes to the bee, so too did Xander. This made it even more special to our school and Saffie's friends.

The Little Superstar was complete and looked stunning. We sent it back to the organisers in Manchester, with the following caption to be displayed both with the bee and on the marketing materials to reflect the inspiration behind the design. It read:

The bee is inspired by Saffie-Rose Roussos, who sadly lost her life in the Manchester Arena attack. Children from her year group at Tarleton Community Primary created it with the help of friends from two other schools: Tarleton Holy Trinity and All Saints Hesketh with Becconsall. While the bee celebrates Saffie's life, it also celebrates communities coming together at difficult times. Love conquers all.

We soon found out that Saffie's bee would be displayed in Manchester Cathedral, a fitting place for it, considering the grandeur of the building and that it was also the location of her funeral, where so many lovely things were said about her.

We organised to take a small group of Saffie's friends to Manchester to find the bee and complete the bee trail. It was a preview of the artistic festival that would open fully days later. Janette led this trip, with another teacher, and met the children at Preston train station early one summer's morning. The children arrived with their parents to drop them off. The children were quiet and looked a little apprehensive, something they shared with their parents who looked equally anxious. They travelled to Manchester and the staff noted that they were more clingy than normal, some wanting to hold the hand of an adult. At this stage they would have been ten years old, so this was more unusual at this age, but obviously the staff obliged, giving them comfort and reassurance.

Initially, they had been given the wrong instructions and had been taken to a large warehouse where the giant bees, four times as large as The Little Superstar, bee were located. The staff and children put aside their initial frustration at being wildly out of location to sweet-talk themselves into this off-limits place and explore these bees, taking photos and posing with them, and simply looking at all the creative ways the professional artists had completed their work.

From here, the staff took them to Manchester Cathedral to find their bee. Some of them would have attended the funeral just under a year previously, so returning so soon must have been challenging. They were keen to find their bee, despite there being many others dotted around the cathedral; they didn't need to try too hard as it was located very near to the main entrance. Their reaction was of initial quietness as they carefully assembled themselves around the bee. There was a sign clearly saying not to touch any of the bees, but this was disregarded and, sensing the mood, the teachers allowed them to continue as they sat around it. The children were very reflective and emotional, with some of them crying openly. The staff managed this well and, after providing them the time for a momentary pause, they suggested lighting some candles if they wanted to, helping them to focus on happy thoughts about the fun times they had spent together with Saffie. This supported the children, and they all lit a candle. All in all, the group spent an hour in the cathedral. After lighting their candles, they searched for the other bees, but wanted to return to the Superstar bee before leaving as they were upset that they wouldn't see it again. They were reassured that the bee would fly back to Tarleton after the festival and that Mr Upton was having a cabinet built to display it. It still proudly sits there to this day, an important part of our school history.

The party were feeling very flat, so they had a picnic lunch in the cathedral grounds before they plotted a route to find lots of other bees in locations around the city. Janette made the decision that they really needed to lift the children's moods, so they made it a light and fun afternoon with photos of silly faces and laughter, as well as an impromptu trip to a café at Piccadilly Train Station (we had been careful in our planning not to go via Victoria) for drinks and ice cream. The day had been a success, and again had supported the well-being of this group of children who were clearly loved by our staff.

Alongside Bee in the City, we were also planning our very own Festival of Peace. This was an event I had had in my mind from our contact with the Japanese Embassy. I wanted to create a community event led by the children from our local schools that focused on peace in a variety of ways. We would set up an art exhibition as part of it, using the pictures that had been gifted to us from the embassy and children of Japan. In my mind, it would have been a real shame not to use them in such a positive manner, as they had been a catalyst for this whole event. I selected a perfect venue, which was the Hesketh Bank Christian Centre. It had a large, modern, and well-equipped hall for the performances, as well as a large reception and café area. We would set up this area as an art gallery, not only to display the work of the Japanese children, but also our own children's artwork, as I had given them a challenge to look at the construction of the pictures and try to produce similar images. Another bonus of the venue was that it was led by a team of highly skilled, caring people who always went the extra mile for their community, which included our school.

The other local schools that formed our cluster supported the event too, so that on the night we had an array of performances including poetry, drama, choirs, and brass, all playing to celebrate the peace we were so privileged to have in this country. There was even a fashion show, with an array of T-shirts promoting peace, and it was funny to watch some of the boys in particular strutting their stuff on the catwalk. I had invited Peter Heginbotham, the honorary consul for the Japanese Embassy, to the event. However, by this stage he had retired from his role.

The event again helped our children in their recovery. The buzz a good performance gives you fills you with endorphins, and when coupled with a community coming together, you cannot help but feel the care that was clearly in that room. I was grateful to all the staff from all the schools for supporting us and making it such a special evening, despite it being incredibly warm and sticky in the hall due to the number of bodies and the short, sharp, heatwave we were experiencing.

Chapter Twelve

There are points in life where you can do something or do nothing. It is a fork in the road, to either address issues or ignore them. While I led the school through a sustained period of recovery with very visible support for the school community, behind the scenes I wanted to address the issues we had faced initially as well as those that presented themselves on our journey. Moreover, we wanted to share our learning to support others.

The catalyst was the six-month anniversary of the attack, and I was miserable. After singing with the children, I hid myself away in my office. It was the day that I responded to those kind people, schools, and organisations, all of whom had made donations to us and that I had the contact details for. It made me feel better to send a letter of thanks to them all. They probably wouldn't have expected it, and many months had passed, but it felt like the right thing to do. I also took the opportunity to send two other letters. The letters were almost the same in content but reflected on the issues that had arisen at our school over the last six months, in the aftermath of the terror attack, and made recommendations about areas to improve. The purpose of the letters was to ensure that schools were better supported in the future, should they face a similar issue, and that there could be lessons to be learned from what had happened to us. I couldn't bear for anyone else to go through what we were going through alone. I felt that our school, staff, and children had been let down by the people who should have checked in and helped us, namely the local authority and the government. The letters were sent to the Chief Executive of Lancashire County Council, as well as the Right Honourable Theresa May MP, who was the Prime Minister at the time. One letter had a much greater impact than the other, but I was pleased that the many writing lessons I had taught over the years, as a class-based teacher discussing the power of the pen, would eventually pay off. I wrote:
Dear Prime Minister,

I am writing as the head teacher of Saffie-Rose Roussos, the youngest victim of the Manchester bombing, as today marks six months since the tragic event. This morning we held a special assembly to mark today and I can tell you that the grief is as raw now as it was six months ago. The purpose of my letter is to provide you with some recommendations for your government to consider to safeguard the well-being of school communities in the aftermath of a terror attack. As the only primary school in the country to experience this, I feel well-placed to do so, however, I am sure headteachers of schools linked to Grenfell Tower will have their own experiences in dealing with a tragedy in such exceptional circumstances.

Saffie's story became a real focus for the press, who were at times very intrusive, as she was the youngest victim and because her mother and sister were also damaged by the bomb. I also feel that, because Saffie came from a hard-working middle-class family, children's innocence was stripped: as, if it could happen to Saffie, it could happen to them. As I am sure you can imagine, given your highly stressful job, the death of a pupil in such circumstances and the aftermath is a highly stressful and emotive issue for school leaders and schools to deal with.

Recommendations:
Debrief
At no point has the school been approached by our local authority (Lancashire) to gather views on and share learning from this event to support other schools should another attack happen. A debrief would have supported school leaders' well-being. It could also have looked at further support for the school.
I would recommend the government to make this a statutory responsibility of a local authority.

CIST
Lancashire have a Critical Incident Support Team. This consisted of two educational psychologists who supported us to a certain degree; however, this was unprecedented, and I feel there should be a greater depth within the team, and this should be available in the coming weeks and months after an incident. For example, staff needed supervision, pupils counselling,

parents counselling/workshops. A great help would have been a well-being worker assigned to the school whose knowledge of services and accessing/signposting support would have had a significant impact.

I would like the government to consider ensuring every school in the country has access to a Critical Incident Support Team and that they are made up of professionals who can advise schools on Counselling, Well-being, Prevention and Early Help, Finance, Prevent, Faith, & Supervision.

Financial Advice
To date, £13,047 has been received by the school as a memorial fund. This was something that we did not set up, but contributions started to roll in following the intensive media coverage. A plan to support schools, including the pitfalls, would be of benefit as would a face-to-face meeting with a finance officer. Doing the right thing with the money is a challenge for school leaders and has been very stressful.

I would recommend that the government supports schools in using the correct processes when dealing with finances following the death of a pupil. This could be in the form of publication from the Department for Education.

Financial Support
A nominal fund, i.e., a crisis fund. This would be funding that can be released quickly to ensure headteachers are able to support the well-being of their community without needing to call on favours from organisations. I feel that in a time where local authorities are diminishing around the country, this would be best served straight from the Department for Education.

This could be used for specific counselling and may extend beyond the children in the school to children in other schools. For example, we work as part of the TaRDis cluster of schools and accessed support from Child Action North West which we opened up to all children and their families in the local area with the rationale that they are all Lancashire children.

We have also included pupil and staff well-being on our School Improvement Plan, in particular Growth Mindset, and this ongoing type of work will be vital for our children. Training could have come from a crisis fund as the children at our school will carry the loss of a friend for the rest of their lives.

I would recommend that the government establishes a crisis fund for schools to deal with the aftermath of a terror attack.

Supervision
External supervision of staff would have been greatly appreciated. To illustrate how dangerous situations like this can be to an individual's mental health and well-being, I would like you to consider my role. As a head teacher, I supported the staff to get them back into class and then ensured ongoing support, dealt with the world's media (some of which were very intrusive), was on news reports around the world, quoted in newspapers and social media, liaised with Saffie's family, internet trolls, in eleven sittings broke the news of a child's death to two hundred and seventy-six children, supported parents with how to talk to their children about death, received a range of requests to support the school – some of which were not appropriate, gave the eulogy at Saffie's funeral, identified and supported pupils as well as run the school which is at times a very stressful job. In my personal life, my wife was 37 weeks pregnant. For some head teachers, the multitude of all these factors would have resulted in them being very unwell. I am lucky to have an understanding and supportive network of family and friends. It is vital that we look after school leaders (as well as other staff) who are an expensive resource if off on long-term sickness absence.

I would recommend the government to make supervision of school leaders following an incident a statutory responsibility of a local authority.

Support for Muslim Children
Our school is predominantly made up of White British pupils. We have a small number of children of Muslim faith. In this particular incident, we have seen pupils deeply affected as they questioned their own beliefs and were fearful of people thinking they supported terrorism. These anxieties are clearly unfair for

the Muslim faith to bear and I feel further work needs to support children's identity following an incident of this magnitude and in these circumstances. For schools with a high proportion of pupils from the Muslim faith, additional money would be needed to support specific interventions.

I would recommend the Department for Education consider running a pilot project to support children from the Muslim faith following an attack by Islamic terrorists.

Prevent

Information from colleagues in Manchester schools was that police had warned them that there may be an attack targeting an educational establishment. At the time, Tarleton Community Primary was probably the most well-known primary school in the country due to the media attention. It would have been helpful for a Prevent worker/officer to come to the school and work with school leaders to ensure appropriate lockdown procedures were in place and offer advice and guidance in this area, as we were swamped with everything that we were dealing with.

I would recommend that part of the national Prevent strategy encompasses further work with schools to address specific issues.

Strategic Support Meeting

All these issues could have been addressed within seventy-two hours of the attack with a meeting in school with the right people sitting around the table: Police, School, Press Liaison, Wellbeing Prevention & Early Support worker, Local Authority, Finance Officer as well as other parties that would be relevant. An action plan would be drawn up and another meeting would then be timetabled to review actions. This process would continue until the school felt they no longer needed it.

I would recommend that a Strategic Support Meeting becomes a statutory requirement for schools affected by a terror attack.

I would like to thank you for taking the time to read this letter and hope that you will be able to consider my recommendations.

Yours sincerely

114

Sending the letter had released some of my frustrations, and I hoped that it would be read and consideration given to my thoughts and recommendations. A few weeks later, I received a response from 10 Downing Street. It came from Lord Theodore Agnew, who at the time was the parliamentary under-secretary of state for the school system. He responded positively to my letter and a meeting was set up with representatives from the Home Office and Department for Education early in the new year.

At a similar time, I received an email from the local authority in response to the letter I had sent to the then executive director. It was from a senior member of the School Improvement Service and somebody that I knew well and respected. The letter had been passed to him and he wanted to arrange a visit to the school, also in the new year, for himself and another senior colleague from Lancashire County Council's Health, Safety and Resilience Team. It appeared that the letter had struck the right chord and that finally, after all this time, the local authority was willing to listen to us and perhaps take some learning forward from what had happened to us as an organisation in the aftermath of the bombing. Since the departure of the Critical Incident Support Team on the second day, our school adviser had continued to touch base with us, but nobody in a senior position had written to us, telephoned us or set foot in the school. No one had asked how the staff or children were. These were Lancashire children and staff who were on Lancashire's payroll, and nobody seemed to be bothered. This annoyed me intensely – they had dropped the ball. I also found it rude that the then executive director had passed the letter down the food chain without a response in person. It was certainly a lesson in leadership of how not to do things. I firmly believe that if you are working in a career in the public sector, your pay cheque shouldn't supersede your sense of duty. That said, his response included a comment that he had spoken to our school adviser about some of our thoughts many months ago and that these were shared with colleagues at the local authority. While this was positive, it also drew the question: 'Why have they done nothing with that information?' They probably just saw me as a nuisance and hoped that I would go away. We arranged to meet at the start of the spring term in the January.

In contrast, at the end of the week when the attack took place, I was out and about around the school when a lady from the office told me there was a phone call. It was Tracy. 'Who's Tracy?', I asked, as the response was a little vague. After a bit of a shrug, I was told that Tracy was the personal assistant to Sir David Carter. I decided that I had better see what Tracy wanted as it might be important. Tracy was warm and bubbly with a thick southern accent. She explained who she was, then put me through to David. If I am honest, I didn't have a clue who he was at the time. As he pleasantly introduced himself to me, I quietly typed his name into Google, trying my best not to alert him to the fact I was typing - I really didn't want to appear rude. Google quickly came up with the search results: David was the National Schools Commissioner at the Department for Education, with an impressive C.V. around leading schools. From the picture, he also had great hair. Despite the many accolades he had, David came across as a lovely man. He explained that he was calling on behalf of the Department for Education to thank me for my leadership that week and for my leadership in the weeks ahead. He was very keen to know how the children and staff were, and at that stage as well, whether or not there was any further support that we needed. I believe that he had taken the time out of his busy schedule to contact the leaders of all educational institutions who had been affected by the bombing. It was a nice touch and incredibly well received. I am sure, like me, other leaders felt valued by this contact at the end of the toughest week in all of our careers. It was just a shame that my own local authority, at the higher levels anyway, didn't have the decency to look after one of their own schools. I am sure that a neutral observer would point out there was a lot going on at the council at this time. A streamlining of jobs with a new upper management structure saw the top team on their way out. There was also a political scandal, with senior politicians arrested over an inquiry into the awarding of contracts. The reality was that it was all very messy and we were far from their thoughts.

As the autumn term was moving towards its finale, Christmas, the school had its usual lovely feel about it. Decorations filled the classrooms and there were various festive arts and crafts adorning the low wooden cupboards at the side of the classrooms, while glitter sparkled from the carpets. We always work very hard, like schools up and down the country, to ensure that we create lasting memories, a family togetherness that always feels so unique in a primary school during the festive season. This year wasn't any different, but it felt so important to achieve that. There was ongoing support for targeted children, but the excitement of Christmas did give a little bit of respite to the inner turmoil some were facing.

One of my pet hates at this time of year is the annual Christmas card from our local MP. This is certainly nothing against the MP themselves, but the principle of collectively, across all the constituencies, spending vast sums of money on buying the cards and then the postage to send them to various constituents. If you consider this for every MP, you are talking a lot of money. As a head teacher working in an underfunded education system, little things like this get to me. This particular Christmas, the card, or should I say the insensitivity of its theme, deeply upset and offended me. I opened it expecting to see a winter's scene, perhaps a snowman or Father Christmas, but was met by the picture of a scene from Syria on the front, a young goat herder tending to his animals in the middle of the war-torn town of Azaz. There was even a tank in the picture. I sat staring at it in total confusion. Was this some kind of sick joke? I opened the card to see that it was from our local MP. In their defence, it was a charity card for the Hands Up Foundation with the aim of reminding their friends in Syria that they had not been forgotten and to celebrate the resilience of the people of Syria. However, I found this hard to see from the picture, and could only draw my own interpretation of what was going on. When you consider that Saffie's murderer had completed his terrorist training in Syria, seven months after her death, you couldn't have picked a worse card. I accept that people make mistakes and again, we were not the top of the MP's priorities. I wrote to her to point this out, but received no response. Friends of the Roussos family also put me in touch with her assistant, but again there was no response. In her position, I would have been mortified and gone out of my way to apologise to the head teacher of a primary school in my constituency whom I had offended, especially as I had named the little girl who had died in my election acceptance speech. We were simply ignored. At no point did she make contact with the school at all to check in and see if there was anything that we needed, not even in passing at the One Voice One Love concert, which I often found strange. I had previously written to her to point this out, but my very direct letter was ignored too. You can allow these little issues to eat away at you, but they can become a distraction, and as we entered a new year, I needed to let it go and focus on continuing to support my school community in what was going to be another difficult year.

With the new term underway, we soon had our scheduled meeting with the local authority. The two gentlemen met Janette and I in my office, and it was a friendly meeting, which was what I had hoped for. They had the letter I had sent in their hands and we talked through the points that I had raised. It was useful in terms of the insight we were given about the complexities that local politics and information sharing had caused, due to the various layers of bureaucracy and numerous agencies and local authorities being slow to talk with one another. The North West of England has many local authorities and services, and this would probably have been an issue regionally around the country. The issue with the Manchester bombing itself was that it was a concert at the Manchester Arena. As one of the principal venues in the north of the country, music lovers had come from miles around. If you consider what is geographically between Manchester and Glasgow, you will see that there are a lot of people who, if they want high-class live music, need to travel. Ensuring services and a response, not only across the North West but really all over the country, was always going to be a challenge, and we were all pieces in that jigsaw. Following a talk I had given at a Prevent conference, where I had discussed concerns about support from the police, a member of the Lancashire Constabulary had shared that they hadn't supported our school because they had been told by Greater Manchester Police that they, GMP, were taking the lead on it something that never happened. This explains some of the confusion in the aftermath of the attack.

Notes were made in the meeting and, as the two gentlemen left, there was a promise that it would be written up and shared with us before being used with different elements of the local authority as learning to support them moving forward. Both Janette and I felt pleased that we had achieved something, as we have both always considered that part of our role in all of this misery was not only to support our children, staff, and community to get through it, but to share our own experiences in order to help others. We were doing this now.

As the months passed, we never received the write-up from our meeting, that learning that we were so desperate to impart to others. I felt quite awkward about it, but I had to follow it up with them because I believed that our experiences were not going to be brushed away. I very much considered that they had come to the school to pay us lip service in the hope that we would disappear. So, five months after the meeting, I chased them with a polite email to see where everything was up to. The one-line response that I received irritated me intently, 'What made you think of this this windy morn?' It may well have been meant in a friendly manner, but given the subject matter, it simply wasn't OK. Janette told me off for my sarcastic response, which was: 'I was just looking out my window, wondering where the local authority were.' Probably a little childish and not the most professional response I have ever sent, but it set the tone for further correspondence. This ended in an apology and further information that what we had shared had been fed into a real-time exercise with the police and army, as well as local authority planning in this area. They simply didn't have the capacity to write it up. I really hoped this was the case but still felt a little fobbed off. I would park the issue, for now.

Chapter Thirteen

At a similar time to the meeting with the local authority, we also received our visitors from the Home Office Victims of Terrorism Unit and the Due Diligence and Counter Extremism Division from the Department for Education. I'd never really dealt with people directly from these areas of government before, and when I had initially received Lord Agnew's letter of response of behalf of Theresa May I had had an image of Thomson and Thompson, from the Tintin books, visiting us. Two middle-aged men in dark suits and bowler hats, with canes. The reality was miles away from this, and two engaging and interesting ladies joined Janette and I. Again, it was all very relaxed, and we were able to talk comfortably about our experiences and what we thought needed to change. They were both skillful at eliciting information from us. At last, someone was listening and seemed to genuinely care and want to make the difference that could support others. We discussed every point that I had made in my letter and were able to evidence our thoughts through our firsthand experiences. Sitting there, talking about everything from the past eight months, reminded me of what a unique situation we were in. When I considered what had happened and what we had initially put in place, and everything else we had done to get to this stage, I realised that it had been an almost impossible journey. There was no guidance to refer to and minimal support, but there should have been. It made me happy that the conversation moved to our recommendations and the production of some form of advice or guidance for schools about what to do in the aftermath of a terrorist incident, that could be a starting point for other schools or educational organisations if they found themselves in the unlikely and unfortunate situation we had found ourselves in.

My warmest memory, which may seem a strange comment given the subject matter, was that, as the meeting neared its end, the lady from the DfE asked, 'Is it OK to look round the school and check in with the staff and children?' I was delighted, as was Janette. Kindness is such a simple thing, but these ladies had come all the way from London and wanted to see our school and our school family. It really meant a lot, especially with how we were feeling about things at a local level. As we toured the school, they both chatted away to the children and staff, getting a good feel for the school, probably gaining further context to what we had talked about. They both had a lovely sense of humour, which they needed when one of our teachers got confused and, in a friendly manner, asked them if they were here for the teaching job we had advertised at the time. She was mortified when she found out who they were.

Their visit started a strong professional relationship between the school and the DfE Due Diligence and Counter Extremism Division in particular, and we would always be open to supporting them through sharing our learning from the experiences we had faced. On some occasions, I would be telephoned and asked my advice on certain matters, especially if they were setting up to work with those of us who were victims of terror through our organisations. I suppose I was a bit of a sounding board at times, maybe because I was so open about everything and just never wanted to see another school go through what we had gone through.

The letter that I had sent to the Prime Minister on the six-month anniversary of the attack had had real impact in terms of it being a catalyst for a wider piece of work to ensure a conversation was had regarding preparedness in educational settings. This would be ongoing across many months and built into a strategy. Following our visit, other educational establishments also shared their learning from their own unique circumstances and the learning was listened to, considered, and collated. The importance of this work should not be underestimated. Understanding how to be prepared following a terrorist incident will not affect many people or institutions; however, if it supports just one school or college and helps children, young people, or staff then it is a job worth doing.

The information we had shared always seemed to be held in high regard and we have always received regular updates about its progress. On one such occasion, two members of the DfE team came back to the school to share their final findings. It was another positive meeting and they shared with us that they were preparing a form of checklist to support schools and colleges in the aftermath of a terrorist incident. Janette and I both felt pleased that the information that we had shared would in some way go to helping other people, although, deep down, we hoped it would never be read because nobody else would need it. An unrealistic view, but well-intentioned. We were told that the checklist was currently with ministers to be signed off and that it would be released in due course. Driving home that night, I felt satisfied but also quite emotional. It was a win for our school, staff, and, most importantly, our children, as despite what everyone had been through, we were helping others – moral purpose is the glue that holds society together.

A month later I received an email with the checklist. It was part of a wider document called the School and College Security Guidance. As I flicked through it, I saw that many of the recommendations we had discussed were in it: press intrusion; mental health support; consideration for members of communities linked to perpetrators; exam considerations; and financial support and advice. The advice would make leaders think about approaches and what might be heading their way.

In the years that followed, further work was completed in this area behind the scenes at the DfE, such as the Victims of Terror working groups where elements of the letter were shared and the learning from our experiences discussed, as well as that of other educational institutions. Colleagues reflected that this had enabled them to better support education settings in other, more recent, terror attacks. There was also work with counterterrorism policing, to look at ways to train regional coordinators with a view to improving messaging across the education sector. The power of the pen is an incredible thing, when coupled with people who are passionate about what they do and about making a difference, as our colleagues clearly were. I was proud to work with them.

At a similar point in time, I received, like other Lancashire head teachers, a notification from the local authority explaining that they had changed the offer of the Critical Incident Support Team. I had always been dubious of the response given to me that information had been passed on from our meeting, as the proof would be in the pudding as to whether there would be visible change. There wasn't any. The notification explained that

CIST had changed its name to become CIPFA (Critical Incident Psychological First Aid), and provided an explanation that appeared to drastically water down its offer, in that it was now a telephone consultation service for head teachers, in the event of a traumatic incident which was affecting pupils, that was provided by the Lancashire Educational Psychology Service. It would provide initial information on trauma, give practical advice on the initial school response to any given situation, and would signpost leaders to appropriate services or organisations. It seemed such a long way away from what it needed to be and what we had shared. It may well be that this would fit the needs of many schools, dependent on the situation, but there were huge gaps in how the local authority would support their schools and children. No mention of a wider scope than educational psychologists, of longer-term targeted support, of financial advice, of a team of professionals and single point of contact for a head teacher, to take the burden off them from the groundwork that would need to be accomplished.

Reading the changes made me feel angry. They had taken a service which, in my opinion, lacked depth and expertise in a high-profile situation such as Saffie's death, and made it worse. It was a service provided by the team of educational psychologists, who at this point were few in number, and I could only imagine was a decision taken due to their workload and potentially the county's finances. There was no way that a school would be well supported if another attack or something else of that magnitude should happen. I emailed the team leader for our area of Lancashire for further clarification, explaining our background, views, and the meeting with the two senior colleagues that we had held. I asked: 'Were our views ever shared and considered? Why has a new model been put in place? In terms of the local authority supporting schools in the wake of a terror attack, what has changed since 22 May 2017, in Lancashire?'

Four days later, I received a holding email telling me that they needed to find out further information and would get back to me shortly. Having heard nothing over two weeks later, I chased it up in an email and was responded to a week later. When the response finally came, the team leader explained that the offer had changed due to a need to fulfil the remit of the educational psychology team, as this had been blurred in the past, with schools not fully understanding what CIST was. Schools may have made contact about the expected death of a member of the school community, which wouldn't be a critical incident as schools should have planned for this. I couldn't disagree with the need for clarity, but perhaps this opened the question up that, if schools were misunderstanding these issues, what work was being done to signpost and support them in these situations?

The biggest kick in the teeth was reading that the learning we shared with the two gentlemen from the local authority was never shared with the CIST. They simply knew nothing about it. The team leader had even checked with her line manager who, as the head of the county's Inclusion Service, hadn't had a conversation with either of them regarding this. It appeared that, in taking such a difficult issue to our local authority, giving our time and effort to the greater good while under the cosh, we were simply being fobbed off. She couldn't answer my last question regarding what had changed since 2017 with regard to the manner in which the local authority would support schools in the wake of a terror attack. It was a fair response: you don't know what you don't know, and I respected her for that. The fact she had gone back to her team prior to giving me a reply reflected that no one knew. This fact answered my question in its entirety. It was interesting to note that a member of the Educational Psychology team had started to attend some meetings with a focus on terrorism and extremism.

I couldn't help but feel fed up. Some local authorities are huge machines, with people coming and going. They are used to people complaining and know how to slow this down, to ignore them and discount their views through closing ranks for their greater good. Most people wouldn't have blamed me for giving up on this issue at this stage, but I had one more roll of the dice. My silver lining came in the form of a new Executive Director. She was new to the authority, a veteran of many other local authorities, and was a sharp, determined person who didn't suffer fools gladly. While this brought much trepidation to the ranks in County Hall, at this stage, head teachers from across Lancashire were quietly delighted to see strong, honest leadership that focused on making the work of the local authority, in terms of schools and children, much better. She was also someone who didn't hide behind systems or play games with you. For someone in such an important and busy role, you could contact her directly and she would get back to you almost instantly. I had met her initially at a head teacher residential for a cluster I belonged to. She had come to meet us all to explain her vison and answer questions. There were over twenty head teachers in the room when another presenter said something controversial. The look the presenter received could have cut glass, and initially silenced the room, before she followed it up with the comment that let everyone know who the boss was. We all knew our place, even the most hardened of us. Secretly, we thought she was great, and hoped she would bring to an end to the boys' club mentality of certain areas of the local authority.

So, there I was, sitting in my office, seventeen months after the bombing, still full of the huge disappointment around the lack of support for my children and staff from the local authority who, as an institution, appeared to have fobbed us off. Still wanting to do something positive in effecting change for others in our county, I started typing an email to the new director, as I believed it would make a difference. I wrote telling her my concerns about the current level of support for schools based on our experiences and how it seemed that, by reaching out to them, we had been ignored. And, therefore, our children had been ignored too, some of them suffering greatly, and this was unacceptable. I expressed my disappointment that we never received any communications from the Lancashire executive at the time, leaving us alone to deal with the very many issues by ourselves. I shared the fact that the Executive Director didn't respond to my letter in person, passing it over to two of her senior leaders, who met us but didn't follow up the information we had shared or pass it on to the right people to effect change – we'd been fobbed off. There were so many elements included in that email that I believed still needed to be addressed, in particular the issue of what the current support would look like for schools now. I ended my email with the following:

In conclusion, I know you are currently reviewing different areas within the local authority. In my opinion, we have been

125

dealt the same old Lancashire cards: ignored from on high, delegated to staff to quieten a head teacher on what is clearly a sensitive issue, information not being shared and everyone seemingly too busy to care, as well as covering themselves.

Please could I ask that you consider our initial letter and get someone to answer the question: in terms of the local authority supporting schools in the wake of a terror attack, what has changed since 22 May 2017 in Lancashire? If the answer is nothing, we need to effect change as, should another incident occur, we would have failed children, staff and schools, which is totally unacceptable the second time round.

I was right to send the letter as, impressively, a response came back almost instantly. It was compassionate and reflective. Most importantly, it was reassuring, and I finally felt that our voice was being heard. By this stage the executive leadership in Lancashire was much stronger, with Angie Ridgwell taking on the top role of Chief Executive Director. I was reassured, from the email response, that Angie responds to all letters of this magnitude in person, and that something as serious as the aftermath of a terrorist attack would have been her first priority.

At one stage, many months after the meeting with the local authority, I had received a letter from Angie Ridgwell telling me that I had been nominated for a Lancashire PRIDE Award by a member of the public for my response and leadership to the attack. She did at this point thank me and express that, as I was a teacher, I wasn't eligible for the award. Regardless, it was kind of her to make contact with me.

The email also went on to reflect on three critical incidents that had occurred in the county since the new director had taken up post, each of which she had taken a personal overview of. Finally, she apologised for the failings of the two gentlemen in writing up their notes.

I can't tell you how much better I felt from the information contained in the email, and how relieved I was that finally schools were getting a better deal and a better response from the local authority. In the final part of the email, I was asked to meet with her, along with some governors, to discuss the matters in my letter, and we set a date for the following month.

The meeting occurred on a rather cold and damp November evening which, coincidentally, was also our Parent's Evening. From the correspondence I had received from her personal assistant, I knew two things. Firstly, she was important, as I had had to reserve her a parking space. The only other person I had ever done this for was David Walliams. Secondly, it might be a slightly awkward meeting, as she had summoned one of the gentlemen from the previous meeting to join us, his other colleague being unavailable. He, of course, was early. As we sat in the room together, alongside my Chair, Vice Chair of Governors and Janette, I could see he was nervous. He made small talk, shifting from side to side, and was very red. We didn't want him to be uncomfortable. We all went out of our way to chat to him and make him feel relaxed. He had jointly dropped the ball on this issue, but that didn't make him a bad person. The meeting was about a discussion, then about moving on – I needed this to be the case more than anyone, as did Janette.

The director joined us and, as all participants were present and correct, we started the meeting. I probably came across as a little too direct at the start: a blessing at times, a hindrance at others. This wasn't intentional, but I asked him what he had been doing since our meeting. The director jumped on this immediately, using some very long words that I had never heard of, and set some parameters for the meeting, which in hindsight was useful and ensured it was a better discussion. Some of his responses were interesting. I felt there was a bit of blagging going on, but by some simple questions, we were able to pin him down to answer us properly.

By the end of the meeting, we had put our point of view across and listened to the response, which reflected on the differences of how the incident would be dealt with now in comparison to in 2017. It was more about how people would deal with it, rather than systems, and therefore this would only work in the short term, while those people were in post. The director was certainly skilled and managed the conversations well; it was a difficult topic. A line was drawn: however, I would reflect that I came out of the meeting having put across what I needed to put across. But the feeling I had, as did Janette and the governors, was one of confusion. It was like getting into a disagreement with your wife.

When you start, you have a clear point of view, but by the end, you feel almost sorry and in agreement with her. This felt similar. Fair play to her: she was far more experienced in this area and certainly more intelligent than I was. The strategy appeared to be to acknowledge the issue and apologise, explain the ways issues had been tackled from their point of view, and then draw a line under it all. It was professional and clinical. As we concluded the meeting and got up to leave, she told me that both myself and my colleagues needed to find a way to move forward now and move on. I took this in the manner it was intended, which was supportive, from someone with years of experience in the area of resilience. But she was detached from it all. When you are dealing with the grief of so many people, it is not as easy as it sounds.

The comment stayed with me that night, causing a restless night's sleep. It churned endlessly in my head. We had done a great job supporting everyone over the past couple of years and we were at a stage where we had, in the most part, ended the support. This was a positive. I think the comment had had the impact on me because it felt as if what we had done was easy, almost throwaway, and it wasn't. Janette felt the same, and we had analysed the comment over a cup of tea following the meeting, asking questions of ourselves. Were we too close to everything to detach from it? Our approach had always been that of being human mixed with our professionalism.

The next day, I travelled by train to Manchester. Through colleagues at the Department for Education, I had been invited to the northern launch of a new charity called the National Emergencies Trust, or NET to use its shorter form. It appeared the charity had been set up following national disasters or incidents such as the Manchester Arena attack. As many different charities and organisations had money donated to them for the same purpose, this may well have led to the money being so spread out across the sector that it might not always get to the right people: those most in need. The purpose of the charity was to be a single point for donations that could then be quickly distributed to those affected. Their vision reflects this: 'An independent body that is trusted to work collaboratively to raise and distribute funds fairly and efficiently at a time of domestic disaster.'

Travelling on the train across the North West, I felt miserable. Last night's meeting remained in my mind, niggling me. The voice in my head continued casting doubt on our approaches, especially on chasing the local authority on the issues we had had. Surely, we were right to do this, for the greater good. I disembarked the train at Salford Central and instantly noticed my error in just coming to the city in my suit with no coat, as the bitter Manchester air hit me. As I made my way across Manchester towards the Central Library, where the event was being hosted, the wind cut through the streets as the city's worker bees ducked in and out of buildings in their lunch hour. I myself ducked into a café just off St. Peter's Square, with an overpowering need to get warm but also to eat something, as it had been a busy morning at school prior to catching the train. I had never been in the Central Library before and, as I approached it, I couldn't help but be impressed by the architecture of the building: a columned portico attached to a rotunda dome structure that may have been better placed in Rome than Manchester. Inside was equally as grand. I had been told to bring my passport as means of identification, due to some of the VIPs who could be in attendance. I knew that at the launch event for the south, which occurred at St. Martin-in-the-Fields in London, the Duke of Cambridge had been in attendance. However, the northern version was a much less celebrity-filled affair, due in part to the government calling a general election and the country being in the pre-election period of purdah, meaning that I didn't need my passport after all.

Entering the Great Hall, I saw people milling around the impressive room, networking. Many of them were linked to various charities and this opportunity for professional networking would have been customary to them. Despite being quite a confident person, I just felt out of place and awkward. I felt more comfortable chatting to the lady who had served me a cup of tea, which was so awful that it was kind of halfway between tea and coffee. I noticed a lady standing by herself, so I struck up a conversation. She was actually the organiser of the event and was very knowledgeable about everything that was going on. The conversation ended with her asking if I wanted to meet the Chairman, General the Lord Dannatt. *Why not?* I thought to myself. It isn't every day you get to meet a Lord, especially one who has been the head of the British Army. I was introduced to him by the CEO of NET, who to my surprise told him that I was the head teacher they had been talking about recently, who had been doing some excellent work in the area of supporting children's mental health. That comment lifted me in an instant, and those thoughts of self-doubt I had been experiencing, following the meeting the day before, eroded. It was a wonderful opportunity to briefly meet him, and he appeared a focused and highly intelligent man. It also meant that I could now enjoy the event a little more. It was hosted by the Sky News presenter Gillian Joseph, and featured a speech from the Mayor of Manchester, Andy Burnham. One of the highlights for me was the Manchester Survivors Choir. I had seen them once before, at a charity football match hosted on the training pitch at the Etihad Stadium, an event I took my family to on behalf of Andrew and Lisa Roussos. It was again wonderful to see that despite all the adversity, they had come together in such a positive way – it was very moving. Following one of the songs, a lady from the choir jumped up onto the stage and gave an impromptu speech. It could only happen in the north of England, and was fantastic. It focused on the impact incidents have, and have had, on the mental health of all of those involved: deep scars. It supported the recognition in the room, and also from the National Emergencies Trust, that these were as important as the physical scars and rehabilitation. It was a light bulb moment in my head: people were getting it. The scars would go on for years, a lifetime in some cases, so we couldn't just move on and let it go. Organisations, professionals, and individuals needed to continue to recognise this, something we as a school had done and would continue to do as and when it was needed. I was right to take the approaches I had, and I could see this clearly now.

Chapter Fourteen

For Saffie's friends, the transition to high school was going to be especially difficult. Their final year at our school commenced, with a visit from the Office for Standards in Education, Children's Services and Skills (Ofsted) after only the first couple of days of term. When I had taken up the headship, it was clear that the school needed a little work – strong leadership and effective systems were the order of the day. We were hugely in the Ofsted window at the time of the bombing and were always looking over our shoulder, despite conversations, I am told, occurring in the background, asking them to hold off their visit. This was a further recommendation I had made as I feel head teachers need to be able to lead their school for a sustained period of time with an exemption following a critical incident, and that exemption should be put in writing. My thoughts were that four terms would have been a sufficient amount of time.

Two inspectors came to the school, and I knew the lead inspector, a large Cumbrian gentleman, who had always been reasonable despite his obsession with school websites, something I am sure he would agree with. There was no way round it: we had to discuss the bombing, the impact, and the support we had put in. This must have been difficult for him, but I was impressed with the manner in which he conducted himself. At one stage, Janette and I came into the room allocated to him for a pre-organised meeting. He looked up from his laptop and told us he was scrutinising the parental feedback from a questionnaire that they had sent out – he'd never seen such support and positive comments for a school. He read a couple out and they gave me goosebumps, as it was lovely to hear what high esteem the school was held in by our parents and community. When the report came out it not only acknowledged the work we had done to support our children, but also focused on the other incredible work around school improvement, as we had also to keep moving forward in this area despite the challenges we faced. The report read:

During your two years at the school you have faced some considerable challenges. You have met these challenges with sensitivity, enthusiasm and drive. Tarleton Community Primary School is a learning community in which pupils feel safe and learn effectively.

Leaders' actions to support pupils, staff and the wider community following the tragic events of the Manchester Arena terrorist attack have been exemplary. They ensure that pupils and staff feel safe in school and that they have a place of normality in which to grieve and learn. This is very much appreciated by parents and typified by a one of many comments made using Parent View: 'Last year, during a very tragic and difficult time, the school did not just help the children; they reached out to us as parents, helping us help our children. Above and beyond what they needed to do.'

Soon after the inspection, at the end of the first half of the autumn term, we took our older children on a trip to France – something they were very excited about. This year we were visiting Normandy, with a strong curriculum emphasis on history and learning about the D-Day landings of 1944. We took the long coach journey to Folkestone on the south coast of England and went through the Channel Tunnel before we continued, completing the French leg of our travels.

There was clearly a potential for upset on this trip due to some of the subject matter that we would be learning about. We visited the beaches, Pegasus Bridge, and other significant places. The children were fine. Despite learning of the fighting and the huge death toll, this was history for them, and in the past. There was no reaction, not until we visited a 360 degree cinema playing a film of the landings. It was loud, as the footage showed the large artillery batteries in action. For some of the children, they were frightened. Fortunately, we had grouped them accordingly and we were able to support them. Another incident occurred at Mont Saint-Michel, where there was a high military presence. We hadn't realised at the time, but the French government considered it a very possible terrorist target itself. Seeing soldiers moving through the crowds, machine guns resting in their folded arms, was too much. Some of the children were terrified and we needed to move them away and back to the safety of the coach as soon as possible. You see, for this small and unique group of children, Saffie's friends, they almost felt that her death was her being personally targeted, and that they too could be a target. At such a young age, the randomness of the attack was difficult to process.

For those children, they still needed a great deal of support. Some of them really struggled with the words 'died' or 'death', as they now had such an enhanced understanding of it for children of their age. Where we as adults would want to shelter children from this, we couldn't; their experiences had taken this from us.

In starting to prepare them for their transition to high school, we identified how they were feeling. There were three issues they were concerned about. Firstly, their upcoming SAT tests, something completed by all Year 6 pupils around the country in their final term in primary school. These would fall a week before the second anniversary. Secondly, the normal transitional fears of Year 6 pupils and what it would be like for them at high school. However, this year there were further considerations: *Who will I go to if I'm upset? How will we mark the third anniversary? Will our teachers understand our feelings?* Thirdly, they were leaving us. We had been a sanctuary for them, where the adults understood how they felt and what they were going through. While it would be difficult to see this cohort leave us, I also believed that they needed a fresh start to support them moving forward.

The SATs testing week came and our main issue was having enough rooms for the children to work in smaller groups, as we had so many of them that may have needed a break at various points in the tests to help them to focus. Incredibly, we were also sent an adviser from the local authority to check that we were running the tests and storing the materials correctly. This was a statutory function of the local authority and the adviser who came looked a little embarrassed. The children could have done without a stranger moving through school, in and out of the testing rooms. She did her best to be as inconspicuous as possible, something we all appreciated. Under the exam system you can apply for compensatory marks for any children going through exceptional circumstances, and I applied for the whole cohort. It was rejected. Many of the children were struggling with these important tests so close to the second anniversary, and I struggled with the National Curriculum Authority's criteria. They felt, because it was an ongoing issue, that they could not support our application and award the marks. They couldn't seem to understand that the trigger was the anniversary itself, and therefore in the future. If you consider, as an adult, how you feel around the time of an anniversary of a loved one's death, I am sure that you will recognise that you are not as productive, as your mind is simply on other things. I just felt that the criteria and processes were not trauma informed and that we were an anomaly in the system. Despite my complaints, they wouldn't budge, so I turned my focus to attempting to get this support for individual children, those who were suffering the most, and I was successful in my approach. It was all about fairness, to me, and was a small win, but I still struggle to understand in the grand scheme of things why they were unable to support our children better – the whole cohort had been affected. In addition, good school data, at this stage, was important. It informed the Ofsted framework as well as the parents' choice of school. By not supporting schools like ours, ultimately, the NCA could have cost us pupil numbers, which are our main source of income. It seems unfair that we could have had a financial penalty simply due to circumstance and doing the right thing by focusing on the well-being and mental health of our pupils at all cost.

With SATs out of the way, we could focus on the two other issues around transition: embracing the new and letting go of the old. Prior to this period, I had been invited to talk at a regional conference in Bury for the Manchester Resilience Hub. It was a useful experience for me, as I shared our approaches and story to a room predominately filled with colleagues from the field of mental health. It also afforded me some good connections to support our ongoing work, and some learning experiences. I listened intently to two engaging educational psychologists, based in the Manchester area, talk about the support they had given to schools. Their support was well focused, targeting need, and wasn't a short fix. I wondered if some of our issues were in part because services focused more predominately on Manchester.

The most humbling part of the day was the release of a new animation the Resilience Hub had made with survivors of the attack, called *A Journey of Recovery*. It had been commissioned by the We Love Manchester fund. The voices on the animation were all young people aged in their late teens. I knew about the animation a few months prior to this, as the lead psychologist had asked my opinion about the resource from the point of view of using it in a school. I had sat in my office, listening to the audio part only, and was very moved.

At the conference, the young people joined us to talk about their experiences, which were also reflected in the animation. It focused firstly on the negative way they had been treated by their schools or colleges, and then the on positive ways. It was heartbreaking to hear what some of them had gone through. Fire alarms going off and the trauma this had caused; an obsession with their attendance from their school or college in the days after the attack; as well as those organisations not being willing to make small changes and allowances for them. On the other hand, other organisations had done a brilliant job of checking in on them, seeing what support they needed, making them aware of routine fire drills, and basically being kind and considerate human beings.

The video had stuck in my head, as I felt it would have real value with the high school when we planned the transition work with them. I arranged a meeting with the head of school and also invited the lead psychologist. We played the animation and he made lots of notes, which was reassuring. I'd known him for many years, and he was a good man, someone who cared about education and the children. I saw the meeting as a real opportunity to nail our colours to the mast about these children and work collaboratively to ensure everything was in place for them in September. It must have been difficult for the high school, as they would be receiving this cherished group of children but would not have the same understanding that we had over the trauma they had faced and were still facing. Perhaps this was a good thing. We created a plan, including additional sessions for selected children, writing out to parents in case there were others still having difficulties at home that we were unaware of. This was the case and we picked up a couple more

135

children. The first contact with the children would occur at our school with Tracy present. Then, a couple of days later, she would take them to the high school, followed by a further visit where they would go with staff from the high school. This approach was successful, although when the last day of term came it was excruciating, I knew we had done our best for them. We also organised and facilitated a meeting between the parents of the children most affected and the high school. It was held at our school and allowed the parents' voices to be heard and concerns looked at jointly, so that the transition would be the best it could be for those children.

The other issue in my mind related to the children's potential vulnerability to developing extremist views as they moved through their teenage years into adulthood. Their best friend had been killed by an Islamic extremist, but that didn't mean the Muslim faith was evil and that everybody was bad. You must understand that there was never an issue around this – not a cross word spoken – but we did have children with deep-seated anger and confusion about the attack. I wanted to put a small project in place prior to them leaving our school, but needed to find the right person to lead it.

I had been asked by Burnley Council, as part of their work on the Prevent Duty, to do a couple of talks across the county. On the second occasion, I met a man called Afrasiab Anwar MBE. He worked for the local authority in different guises, but was also a local politician in the east of the county and had been successful in his work around community cohesion. As a member of the Muslim faith, Afrasiab articulated what it meant to be a Muslim, with an openness about his faith, what it meant to him, and an emphasis on the fact that it was a faith of tolerance and love. I felt that he could really help our school and this particular group of children, sowing the seeds in their young minds and giving them the correct information that they needed to have an informed view.

Afrasiab was delighted to be part of this project and set aside two days to help us. On the first day he did a whole school assembly, explaining his faith, before going to all the other classes to complete workshops where he showed resources and modelled using a prayer mat. The next day we took all the children from Year 5 and Year 6 to a mosque. This should be something very natural for schools to do, but for us it was brave. It was a big step for some of our children, but an incredibly worthwhile visit. The mosque itself was stunning. The children themselves were more fascinated with the minbar and the washrooms than anywhere else in the building, but got involved in the learning and the trip was a success. As we came out of the mosque and waited for the coach, two old ladies approached the children, wearing full burkas. They struck up a conversation, asking the children which school they were from and what they were doing at the mosque. It was lovely to watch: they were all so engaged with each other across their generations, and it was another sign of people coming together. It didn't matter what religion the children or the ladies were; there was respect, and I felt proud. Afrasiab came back to school with us and completed further work with our children. He did a tremendous job for us and we will always be indebted to him. All but one of the parents were supportive of our approach and they opted to find another school.

One of the last events we held with the children before they left our school was the unveiling of a garden that had been created by friends of the Roussos family: a large decking area with a loveheart cut into its centre, with roses in. The roses were dark pink and had been cultivated as the Saffie Rose. These were being sold up and down the country, with proceeds going to charity. It occurred on what would have been Saffie's eleventh birthday. We were joined by a charity called Once Upon a Smile, whom the family had a personal connection to and who offered bereavement services to children. On this occasion, they made teddy bears with the children, the Once Upon a Smile staff using their therapeutic skills to support them. This was followed by the opening of the garden and a cup of tea and a piece of cake in the hall. Andrew produced a huge birthday cake from the boot of his car and the children's eyes opened wide with delight when they saw it. Andrew and Lisa had always shown so much concern for the well-being of Saffie's friends. Their strong relationship with the children, from the many sleepovers and parties that were now years in the past, was clearly evident.

It was the last time Andrew and Lisa visited our school. When they left, they sat chatting to other parents in a way that a lot of Year 6 parents do on the last day of term, year after year. It felt like a change for them, as well as for the children.

Chapter Fifteen

Coming back after another long summer holiday, the school felt different. There was still the occasional issue relating to Saffie's death, but in the main those children most affected had left us. During the Christmas period, Janette and I had popped into a café at the local supermarket for lunch between the various Christmas performances that day. We were met by the Tarleton Academy choir, many of them our former pupils, who swamped us, chatting away and telling us all about their new experiences and asking how we were. It was great to see them thriving in their new school.

Soon after, we were met with further challenges through the Covid-19 pandemic. The skills we had learned over the years equipped us well for this. Just before going into the first national lockdown in 2020, Andrew called to tell me about the Manchester Arena Inquiry and explained that towards the beginning of the inquiry there would be an hour-long pen portrait, an informal description, of each of the victims. He asked me if I would do one for Saffie, which would focus on what she was like in school and the person she could have become. I agreed at once and started pulling some ideas together. To do Saffie justice, I spoke with various teaching staff and made an appointment to visit her old school so that I could find out more about what she was like in her first few years there. When I arrived, I was greeted warmly by the staff, and I sat there scribbling notes as they reflected on Saffie as a young learner. Hearing that she was always late for school there too turned the corners of my mouth up into a smile. I was pleased to have visited the school, as it was important to reflect Saffie at this young age. I only just made it, as a couple of days later, everything locked down. Having written up the pen portrait, I sent it off for submission and didn't really think anything more about it.

Months later, I had managed to get my young family over to Jersey for a summer holiday and was staying at my parent's home when the phone rang. It was Andrew. After our normal small talk and a little banter, he told me that his legal team had asked if those who had submitted pen portraits on behalf of the family would record themselves doing it as, due to the Covid-19 restrictions, this would need to be how it was presented rather than a designated person reading them out as had been previously planned. Having agreed to do it, I started laughing, as I almost knew what was coming next. 'When do you want the recording done by?' I asked. From the reciprocal laugh at the other end of the phone, I knew I wouldn't have much time. 'Monday', came the response. I put the phone down and considered the couple of issues I had. Firstly, I didn't have a copy of the pen portrait with me, but that was easily solved as I could search my emails on my dad's computer and print one off. Secondly, I was standing there in shorts, t-shirt and flip-flops, not the professional presentation I would want to make at such an important hearing. Moving downstairs to the lounge, I approached my dad, looking him up and down. He surveyed me with suspicion. 'What size neck are you?' I asked.

The next day I stood outside my parent's bedroom in my childhood home, dressed in my dad's shirt and tie. On my bottom half I wore a pair of shorts and flip-flops and I ensured that Lucy filmed me from the waist up. I got attacked by a wasp at one stage in the filming, but managed to get through it.

Weeks later, when the inquiry showed the pen portrait, three of us sat in the conference room at school: me, Janette, and Gill from the school office. All of it was a difficult watch, especially listening to some of Saffie's friends and their parents. Everyone involved did an incredible job and I wrote to one of Saffie's friends, a former pupil, to tell her how proud I was of her.

The moving on element, which I had been advised to deal with, was still impossible. My role as Saffie's head teacher wasn't over and my link with Andrew and Lisa was still very much needed. Over the coming months, we were still resolving issues and dealing with heartbreaking situations. We had horrible messages left on our school answerphone that had resulted in police involvement. This was something I initially hid from the family, as I didn't want to upset them, but the police made contact with Andrew. When he called to check we were all OK, I explained my rationale. I suspect he too had had some issues over the years.

I had never heard or even considered the term 're-grief' before. Unlike others, I had been fairly fortunate in my life in terms of the death of loved ones. I had lost both of my grandfathers, but they had lived good, long, honest lives and died in warm beds as part of a loving family – surely that is the way it should be?

While at university, I had lost a close friend who, aged only twenty-one, died of a sudden and aggressive form of testicular cancer. As a fit and healthy young man, whom I had played rugby with and lived with, his death was devastating to all that knew him. His illness lasted only seventeen days from its onset to his death, leaving his devoted mother devastated. I remember that, as a younger man, this had not only brought home to me, for the first time, my own mortality, but had also shown me at first hand the despair of a parent losing a child. It simply wasn't the natural order of things.

The rawness of Saffie's death was, for our community, something that we all felt difficult to deal with, especially for her friends. However, humans are built to find ways of coping, and grief is part of a process in developing strategies to deal with terrible things. We cannot simply remain in a constant state of despair, although I accept that grief can affect you in one way or another for the rest of your life: the image of Queen Victoria in her black dress, grieving the loss of Prince Albert for decades, is a prime example. I also recall a conversation with my own grandmother, who lost her husband and son within a year of each other. She was almost accepting of my grandfather's death. He was an old man who had had his time and had had various ailments over all the years of my lifetime. Although it was upsetting for her, piecing together her own future as a widow, she was realistic about it. However, she never got over the untimely death of her son, my uncle, and it saddened her every day. It is always the little things: those reminders, those messages or phone calls, that are the hardest to move on from. The emptiness of not having that person there is numbing.

Time had passed and it was now over three-and-a-half years since the Manchester Arena attack, a time where I had led my school community through a sustained period of recovery. But with the simple ping of a text message, we were going to be forced to readdress our grief. It was 1 December 2020, and I received a message from Andrew asking for me to give him a call when I could. Within the message he told me that he needed to give me a heads-up, as I could need to put something in place. I normally looked forward to a phone call with Andrew as, through all of this awfulness, a friendship had grown. But I knew the information I was about to hear today could be difficult to listen to. I finished the task that I was working on, then went through to the office next door and flicked the kettle on. After all, I would definitely need a cup of tea. While the water boiled, I had a quick walk around the school to clear my head, limping about. I was experiencing issues with arthritis in my hip and the cool December air was certainly not helping this. Finishing the preparation of my drink, I brought it back through to my office and dialled the number. Andrew answered in his usual manner, pleased to speak to me, and we exchanged pleasantries. The conversation then changed to focus on the Manchester Inquiry, and some information that his legal team would be submitting after Christmas. The family felt this information would cause upset to the school and would need to be dealt with sensitively. Grabbing a pen, I started to make notes, listening intently. I simply couldn't believe what he was telling me. He explained how exactly Saffie had died. Her injuries had potentially been survivable, but there had been issues with the administering of first aid on the fateful night. My notes read:

Injuries knees down
10.31 Bomb
10.38 First aider from arena + public left thought she couldn't be saved
alive/breathing/drinking
10 minutes later nurse/policeman with her
11.00 took her to an ambulance
11.15 hospital
left to bleed to death no injuries life threatening
no pressure etc. put on her legs
11.40 time of death

It is difficult to know what to say at a time like this. I felt such a mixture of emotions. Andrew was just so calm – he had obviously had a long time to consider the information and I am sure that his heart was breaking all over again with having to explain what had happened; his only focus being the truth and doing what was right for his daughter. Someone, somewhere had got it wrong on that night, and not just one person, by the sound of things. Could Saffie have really still been here? I felt confusion as much as any other of the emotions I was feeling. This was such a cruel twist in a story that was already so tragic, the only light being a family who, despite their own feelings, had the best interests of the school and our community at heart. I was thankful to them that they had entrusted me with what was both privileged and confidential information. Andrew had given me the time needed to consider and put together a plan of how I might support the staff and what impact the children may feel, including those close friends who were now at high school and had been for well over a year. The time when this information would be presented to the Manchester Inquiry, and subsequently be in the press, was unknown. From the information that Andrew had, it would be in Section 12 of the inquiry, which would potentially be in the spring of 2021. I was grateful to him for the heads-up, but as I put the phone down, it struck me – what on earth was I going to do?

Staring at the wall for answers, I finished my cup of tea and stared a little longer. Ideas were starting to form in my mind, as well as a lot of questions. The staff team were going to be totally devastated. For the new staff, it was going to be strange. I needed a way to share the news that brought everyone together, as this would be the best approach – we would also need to speak to colleagues in the mental health sector as part of our planning to ensure any support moving forward was in place. It was also important that I was the one to tell them, as the head teacher of our school and someone who had led them through all this horribleness over the years. The Covid-19 pandemic was going to a huge barrier to this.

I had made the decision that the information was to be on a need-to-know basis and therefore I would initially only share it with Janette and Tracy. Personally, even selfishly, I needed someone to share it with who understood how it felt to hear such news. I went into Janette's office and sat down on her spare chair with the tatty cushion that was always perched on it. 'What's the matter?' she asked. Janette and I have been through a lot and she always knows when something is wrong. I would also make a terrible poker player. 'I've got some really bad news and you're going to feel upset and angry,' I responded. She was now eager to know and her eyes widened to receive the information. I recounted the telephone conversation with Andrew as she sat in silence, her face flickering through different emotions, with one predominate feeling pinned there. Anger. When I had finished, she started asking questions, tears streaming down her face. It was horrible, seeing such a devoted colleague and close friend going through this. We both had the same thing on our minds: an hour and ten minutes for a scared eight year to die, to bleed to death. While only one person was to blame for the bomb, how could this happen to a little girl in the North West of England in modern times? We swore a lot. These feelings however, needed to be cast aside. We needed to be both compassionate and professional and consider the staff, children, and our community in what our approaches would be, moving forward.

When you're in the moment, sharing such devastating news with someone, your own survival instincts kick in. You need to get through it just as much as they do while trying to do so in a way that will cause the least amount of distress. I didn't realise at that particular moment, but only when I was driving home, thinking about it later: Janette's reaction was a barometer for how the staff in general would feel, when we shared the information. They were going to feel what we were feeling, and I hated the thought of it – after everything they had done and had been through, they didn't deserve it. No one did.

By the time I had left Janette's office, I had some clarity in my head about my next steps. I wanted to talk to Tracy, as her views as our learning mentor and someone who had worked so closely with the children in the run-up to the first anniversary and beyond were really important to me. This I did, taking a detour on the route back to my office. Tracy had never met Saffie in person, as she had come to the school months after the attack. Strangely, she had got to know her well through the work she had done over the years with her friends, as they recalled different stories about their friend and their feelings towards her and her death. Tracy, like Janette, was flabbergasted at the news.

She also felt that the staff were going to find this difficult to deal with. I had no doubt in my mind that we would need some professional help in the coming months, so I picked up the phone to the Resilience Hub. The lead psychologist answered the phone straight away, which I was pleased about as I couldn't remember whether or not it was a day she worked at the hub. I have always felt reassured by working with her, perhaps due to her attention to detail, eliciting answers from you with her professionally inquisitive demeanour. There were a lot of pauses, a lot of thoughts, and an acknowledgement about how rubbish it all was. We really focused on thinking about how this information could be shared. She recognised that I needed more processing time, and that she needed more time to consider the best ways forward. We arranged a Zoom meeting for a few days later, with the addition of one of her colleagues, as well as Janette and Tracy. This additional time was supportive: there was no need to rush.

A few days later, we all met and discussed the next steps. A slight concern of the psychologists was that, at this stage, they were not aware of any new survivability claims being presented at the Manchester Inquiry. Previously only one of the twenty-two victims had been considered to have had a chance of surviving their injuries. They were being diligent, which was the right thing to do, but they didn't know the family as I did and I had no doubt in my mind that, while there was currently no knowledge of these claims, it would happen. I didn't need any confirmation. This came days later.

When discussing and planning the best ways to speak with the staff, there was one huge elephant in the room: Covid-19. The North West of England had been hit particularly hard during the ongoing pandemic and, having emerged from a so-called second national lockdown, was now in Boris Johnson's tiered system. with the possibility of a stricter lockdown looming ever closer. Everyone could see it coming but the government, it seemed. This was going to make sharing the information tricky, but I desperately did not want to do this by video. So, we discussed my plan. We would set up distanced tables in the hall and invite all the staff in after school on an appointed day. They would sit in the 'bubbles' they were working in (bubbles of children and staff had been grouped, with separate playtimes, and none of them could mix – this was to avoid transmission of the virus), wearing face coverings. I would then talk them through the information, following which they would be directed to four breakout rooms, one for each bubble, so that the staff could have time together discussing the issues that were brought up. Further support would be provided, as we would have a member of the Resilience Hub in each room should they be needed. While it wasn't ideal, it was the best that we could have hoped for given the situation. Everyone in the Zoom meeting agreed that this would loosely form our plan. The next issue was timing. This was tricky, as we needed to strike a balance. We had to ensure that staff didn't hear the new information on the news, but also that we didn't leave too much time between informing the staff and the official release, due to the confidential nature of the information. We attempted to estimate the best time using one of the psychologists' knowledge of when Section 12 could occur. We felt that it was important to park everything until after Christmas, as it had been a relentless term for the staff in schools across the country due to the current national and world crisis. We would reconvene in January to look at dates late in February or early March for putting the plan in place.

Christmas, or some form of it, came and went before we went into another national lockdown early in January 2021. We believed that this would slow down the release of the information to the inquiry as it would result in fewer face-to-face days per week being allowed. This was a rather innocent error on our parts.

I struggle with lockdowns. I suppose it is having your freedom, in part, removed. The options, as you meander through a lazy weekend, stolen from you. This was probably why, on this particular Saturday morning, I had been sent alone to complete the family food shop. I pulled up into Morrisons' car park and checked my phone as, inevitably, I would have left something off the shopping list and would have a reminder about what to pick up. There was only one message and it was from Andrew. The message came really out of the blue and told me two vital pieces of information. Firstly, they had just found out that the independent report about Saffie would be mentioned to the inquiry on Monday, and would therefore be in the public domain.

Secondly, the Roussoses were doing an interview for the BBC tomorrow and it would go live tomorrow night. This was going to be another really difficult time for the family, and I was grateful yet again for their consideration of all of us.

The message did, however, leave me a little dazed, and I tried to regroup and get my head into a more clear and professional mode as I floated up and down the supermarket aisles, list in hand but deep in thought. Although this put me under pressure to share the information, the positive from it was that I no longer had the difficult balancing act over when or how to share it. To respect my staff and ensure that they were hearing it from me and not finding out about it in the media, I would have to share it in the next twenty-four hours or so. In terms of how: we were in a lockdown and it was the weekend. To share the news in person would be against the law, so it would unfortunately have to be done virtually. This was the best I could do and, due to the exceptional circumstances, these were the cards I had been dealt. I would have to move forward with them to the best of my ability.

Driving home, I called Janette, who was surprised that we would have to share the news so soon. But I was determined in my approach and felt that this was the best way forward. As ever, she was supportive, and we decided I would send an email out to the staff when I got home, and that we would have a virtual meeting at 5 p.m. that night. I tasked Janette with making a call to Listening Tree, to speak to Sally or Annie and look at the possibility of organising a virtual group supervision on Monday after school, for those staff who felt that it would be supportive.

Arriving home, I was conscious of the time and the importance of getting the email written and sent out, to ensure everyone saw it. One of the few perks of the lockdown was that everyone was free at short notice. I quickly put together the email and hit send. The email read:

Good afternoon everyone,

I am very sorry to contact you over the weekend.

I have unfortunately got some very distressing news to share with you regarding the Manchester bombing, which will be in the media tomorrow night, that I want you to hear from me rather than happening across it yourselves, as I am sure it will cause great upset to many of us.

I have organised a Zoom for 5 p.m. this evening. This will be less relevant to newer staff who may not wish to attend and you yourself may not wish to, which is absolutely fine. I would please ask for the following protocols:

Be in a room by yourself

Ensure that in particular, no child can hear

Where possible, have a loved one around for after the meeting

The contents of the meeting are highly confidential

The information became apparent in early December but was not due to be presented in the inquiry for a few weeks yet, so it is something I have sat on due to Christmas and the current efforts from everyone in school, but I have been informed this morning that it will break tomorrow in the media; therefore the meeting tonight is out of respect for you all. Could I ask that you message others to ensure they have seen this email?

Best wishes,
Chris

In my haste, I hadn't considered the best means of contacting and inviting members of staff, who had been so affected and been so supportive in May 2017 and beyond, and who had now subsequently left the school over the past few years either to retire or take up another post elsewhere. Such is the nature of schools. Fortunately, members of the team had my back on this and replied asking if it was OK to extend the invitation to them. Of course it was. We had all been through this terrible experience together, and that wasn't going to end now.

The scene was set for 5 p.m., but there was another group that was on my mind – Saffie's friends. There needed to be something in place for these young people, just in case, as we really didn't know what, if any, real impact the story may have in the media. It needed to be handled sensitively. I sat in my study at home and started putting together a list of pupils. By now, they were in Year 8 at high school, so I couldn't reach out directly to them. This wouldn't have been the right course of action in any case, as we needed to speak to their schools to make them aware of the situation and the concerns that we may have had for their well-being. Having compiled a list, I called Janette again and we went through it, adding or crossing off the names of different past pupils until we were satisfied that we had covered everyone who may have struggled. We had identified that the small group of children we were concerned about were at two different schools and, despite being a Saturday afternoon, the head teacher of the first school picked up their mobile phone after a couple of rings. We openly discussed the situation, the children, and our thoughts around it. It was really reassuring to know that they would be able to sensitively reach out to these young people if needed and to keep an eye on them. For the second school, I had never met the head teacher and didn't know the school very well. I was able to get their email address from a colleague and I sent the head teacher an email explaining the situation, including my mobile phone number. Within five minutes my phone rang. It was a lovely, supportive conversation, and again it was wonderful to see the education community coming together to ensure our young people were supported. It was also a great weight off my mind to know that, if needed, the support was there for them and that they wouldn't be forgotten.

When the clock at the bottom right-hand corner of my laptop turned to 17:00, I clicked on 'Start Meeting'. One by one, various staff members joined the virtual waiting room, waiting for admittance into our meeting. There weren't the usual pleasantries exchanged that had become the norm over the last year, as everyone sat in silence. I squinted at the screen, letting everyone into the meeting. I drew a deep breath, then started. I always find that presenting the facts as you have them, in the long run, is the best way forward, however unpalatable they may be. This was certainly my approach here, as I couldn't sugar coat anything; the press weren't going to, and subsequent details would only follow from the inquiry, so I had to give everything I knew to them. While I hope that none of them realised it at the time, there was one part where I really struggled to get the words out. I could see in their faces: the same processing of the facts that Janette had gone through. There were shakes of the head; some were looking down in disappointment; and tears, lots of tears, while the colour visibly drained from some of their faces. What made it stranger was that we were doing it virtually, and, as such, everyone was on mute. There was one voice, and it was mine.

It didn't last long. I felt really helpless, but at least we were in a position to offer initial support, as Janette had managed to organise a group supervision on Monday night with Listening Tree. I hoped that this would help show the staff that we were there for them. I ended the meeting; no cheery Zoom wave. Then I sat there. Staring at the wall, I considered how difficult that had been. It was certainly up there as one of the most difficult things I had ever done. Looking back, stepping out at the front of the school in the initial aftermath of the attack to give the press a statement was difficult. Then, the impossible task of delivering the eulogy at Saffie's funeral was equally so, but, for both of these events, I had had adrenaline pumping through my veins and it had got me through. Over three-and-a-half years later, and in a lockdown, I simply didn't. I was shattered. I know from speaking to staff members about that day in the weeks that followed that they, too, had felt bewilderment and fatigue. One of the worst parts of the day, in some of the staff members' eyes, was the gap between receiving the email and the meeting itself, as they knew they were going to be told something horrendous. Alongside this, there was real concern nationally about the country's mental health, due to the enforced working-from-home rules. Schools remained open to key workers' children, which for my school meant that the teachers were at home, teaching remotely, while the teaching assistants facilitated the learning in school for this small group of children. At this stage, it meant for some of the staff that they were isolated from their colleagues, their friends, and their support bubble. For many, this made processing the news even more difficult. I later found out that some had met up, standing across the street from one another in the open air to have a socially distanced chat as a means of comfort, but it just wasn't the same.

By the time the group supervision came after school on the Monday, people were processing the news. There weren't a lot of us on the virtual supervision, but for those who were, it was useful, and for me it was beneficial to listen to them. A real theme was the ongoing tragedy and how the new information had brought all the feelings that they thought they had dealt with back to the fore. My own reflections were that we had dealt with something truly terrible. A little girl had been murdered in a terror attack, and it was a national story. Over the past few years our brains had tried to sympathetically help us move on, by telling us things like *it would have been quick* or *she wouldn't have suffered*. These coping mechanisms had been shattered. All our worse fears had come to fruition and, on this matter, there was nothing our brains could do about it; the detailed reality was in front of us. While elements of it could be disputed by a good lawyer, the fact was that Saffie had bled to death over a long period of time.

In the few weeks that followed, everything just went silent. There wasn't any further feedback from staff. They were all quietly handling it in their own ways. This troubled me, as normally I would have a pretty good idea of what their needs were, but with many of them working from home, I didn't have a clue about how they felt or where they were up to. I discussed it with Janette, and she had similar feelings. Previously we had discussed doing a session with the Resilience Hub about self-care, and the lead psychologist had very kindly written an open letter to the staff, producing some ideas around how this might look, which Janette had sent out to our team on the psychologist's behalf. There was still very little coming back. Was I getting it wrong? We also had a virtual staff meeting booked with the Resilience Hub, to look at checking in with staff and providing them with information about supporting their mental health and well-being, following the news. This was also important in supporting one another.

At this stage, I didn't want to get it wrong, but I equally didn't want to impose anything on them, as I wanted the session to be beneficial to them. I considered my approach and felt that being upfront and honest was the best way forward, and decided that I would send an email to them, setting out different options, to take away any awkwardness they may have felt at potentially upsetting me. I hoped they would understand that what I was trying to do was coming from a good place. I sent the following email:

Afternoon everyone,

Unfortunately, my illustrious Number 2 is unwell with an ear infection and even more dizziness than normal...therefore I am postponing the staff meeting tonight. So I am directing you to use the time for your well-being. Put your laptops away, relax, walk, eat, drink, and lie in a dark room. Thank you for all you are doing. ☺

Next week we have an hour's session with the Manchester Resilience Hub. This was booked as a support session regarding the information I gave you a few weeks ago in early January. More particularly around having bits in our emotional toolkits to support us, each other, and our community in the coming months as more details emerge.

I am finding it really hard to gauge where everybody is with this as, after the initial shock and anger, everything has gone fairly quiet. While I want to support everyone, I don't want to cause unnecessary distress, so could do with a bit of a steer for the session so that I can chat with the Resilience Hub prior to session, to ensure that it is an effective and well- received session. I also don't want you to feel awkward in responding to me, so we have the following options:

Option A:
Session generally looks at self-care following a critical incident, to keep ourselves safe and each other/children/families.
Option B:
Session looks at self-care, specifically focusing on the issues we are facing, including re-grief, to keep ourselves safe and each other/children/families.
Option C:
You've got it wrong, Chris.
Option D:
Something else (please specify)

Please just respond with A, B, C or D (if you are a new member of staff who may not be affected in the same way as others, you don't need to respond).
Best wishes,
Chris

The email was effective in breaking down that barrier and the staff responded with their views, which were in the most part option B, with a few selecting option A. While I would have received it courteously, as a learning point in the manner it was intended, I was pleased that no one chose option C. It also meant that the session delivered by the lead psychologist was effective and met the needs of the staff. I am so fortunate to work with such a reflective team, and this was really illustrated within the session as we considered how we all felt following the further news relating to Saffie's death. The main theme was that, as a team, it had left us feeling overwhelmed and exhausted, and that the strict rules surrounding Covid-19 had dealt us another blow. Going through the grief process again was harsher when we were not physically together and were not able to have physical contact, such as a reassuring hug. The loss of social contact was really affecting everyone.

Despite my worries, the session was perfectly timed, and helped to equip us with further ideas about self-care, which was as pertinent to our feelings of re-grief as it was to the lockdown. It allowed us to stop to consider our needs, and gave us the time to do so, something that doesn't always happen with school staff. One element I really took away was the notion of an 'emotional bank account', and the question: 'What deposits are you going to make in your account?' I was pleased with how the session had gone; we were there for the staff, they knew this, and I felt reassured that we had been able to come together, as we always had, to support each other.

Following the session, we all went away having acknowledged our thoughts and revisited the issues. Nobody discussed it again. We had processed the information and locked it away in the repositories of our minds, to enable us to continue our journey forward and to deal with the taxing issues the pandemic presented. Emotionally, we couldn't fight on all fronts anymore.

Chapter Sixteen

Just under two years after the attack, I was giving a talk about leading a school though recovery to a group of professionals from various fields of expertise, when one of the delegates asked me how long I thought the recovery process would take. My response came quickly: 'It will take just over four years.'

'Why that long?' you may ask. The response was to do with the children themselves and the resilience of the adults in our school. On telling the children initially of Saffie's death, the children in our younger classes couldn't process it because they were too little – the rest of the children, to some degree, could. We also had a survivor of the bombing in one of the classes, so it was all very real to that child in particular. We would always be ready to support them if it was needed. When I say support, I don't mean the obvious things, but the subtle little things that quietly say to a child, 'The world's not forgotten you' and 'We've got your back.' A check-in or a quiet word before an assembly was important if I felt the subject matter could trigger the traumatic experience for that child. It should also be done in a way that gives the child a choice. When doing an assembly focusing on the 80th anniversary of the Battle of Britain, I was covering topics around bombing, the Blitz, and the devastation that was left. I had told the affected child what the assembly was to be about and, having previously set up an alternative, they could decide if they would join us or not. This is important, because the randomness of terrorism takes away choice, both at the time and for years to come. Regardless of their age, victims do not have a choice in whether they are frightened or not. They do not have a choice in whether to sleep or not at night, while fear and traumatic images sear through their minds and bodies. Giving back control is such an important part of the recovery process.

As the children who needed the most support have moved on from our school, we are now left with the children who were youngest at the time of the attack, and who, generally speaking, hadn't been strongly affected by it. It also means that the staff are no longer dealing with grief and subsequent bereavement issues, which had compounded and delayed their own recovery, and the pressures that we all placed upon ourselves at this difficult and sustained period of time. The staff were truly devastated, but it wasn't until Saffie's closest friends had transitioned to high school and left us that for some, the trauma they themselves had faced really manifested itself in their own mental health. This was felt on a personal level, and we were able to support them through counselling and letting them know that it was OK to feel like that. We are indebted to them, to all of our staff, for the incredible job they have done. Reflecting on it, I believe it shows that they were so focused on supporting the children that, at times, they didn't always recognise the signs that they were affected too. Maybe I should have spotted this sooner, but I didn't. All I could do was my best to support them when they opened up to me, and through the contacts that we had acquired on our journey, I was able to do this quickly and decisively, so that they knew we were fully supportive of them.

The Manchester Inquiry brought up further heartbreak for us as a staff. This was especially the case for those of us following Chapter 12 of the Inquiry late in 2021 as the survivability claim was examined in depth with opposing medical opinions debated. For those of us who knew Saffie, hearing of her injuries in such forensic detail were devastating and difficult to comprehend. However, from the viewpoint of the children, we didn't see any issues directly in school. We were unaware if this was something that was discussed at home or not; parents hadn't told us if this was the case. Perhaps one of the few benefits of the Covid-19 pandemic was that it gave those affected one way or another by the Manchester Arena attack something else that was big and life-changing to focus on. With the inquiry being more restricted in the physical sense, the proceedings were being broadcast on a YouTube channel. People could choose to view this or not, accessing the information they wanted or avoiding the additional pain of discovering something they didn't want to hear, as the specific details could be devastating. The other reality was that the reporting was probably less intense than it would have been in more normal times, as the pandemic had brought with it so much politics from across the world and the UK itself. Everyone had an opinion, from face masks to long drives to Barnard Castle to check your eyes; from opening up the borders to some very expensive and, some may say privileged, wallpaper. The world was moving on, but the families and friends of those affected in the bombing were getting the answers they had so desperately needed for so long. Hopefully, in the long run, this would support them, too.

This was the same for our school. Humans are designed to move on, but also to never forget and to take lessons from the experience. As well as locking Saffie into our hearts, the blue plaque overlooking the playground was testament to the fact that she will always be with us, one way or another.

Just after coming out of the third national lockdown, I led my first bubble assembly in many months, with children in our Lower Key Stage 2 classes aged from seven to nine years of age. They were the children, all those years ago, who were in our youngest class and who had simply wanted to go and play when I told them of Saffie's death. The theme of the assembly was 'Respect', as we were having a few niggles on the playground, the children struggling at times to get on following the many weeks they had spent at home. Part way through the assembly, I was able to talk about Saffie as a role model. 'Does anybody remember a little girl who used to go to this school, called Saffie?' In the main part, they didn't, which was OK: they had been too little at the time. I explained that she had died, but that she was always a role model for us, as when her friends would fall out with each other, she would do her best to help them remain friends. I told them that this could have taken the form of a backflip, or doing the splits while her friends were mid-argument. This made the children in the assembly laugh, and they all took the message away with them.

Reflecting on the approaches I took, I was always mindful that it couldn't be just about getting people through it. There were elements of that, of course, but we needed to ensure that we still gave the children opportunities to have a childhood and be children. So, unapologetically, it was also about finding lots of approaches for them to have fun and to shine. It was layered, and targeted at key times with key groups: sometimes with the whole school, sometimes with small groups or individuals. You have to remember that we couldn't do this in isolation, although sometimes it felt like we were. We needed the help of professionals, who eventually became friends and who were simply amazing human beings. Therefore, giving talks wasn't just about helping others. It was also about my own learning, listening to others, and, most importantly, making those key relationships with people in order to help our staff and children: Colin, Afrasiab, the Resilience Hub, the DfE, and the ladies from Listening Tree being prime examples. They were the real experts in their fields, and I always appreciated their support. While I did have to conduct research around trauma and scour the internet, I am a real people person, so prefer to have those open and frank conversations in person – it really helped me to lead my school effectively.

Finding ways for the children to collectively express themselves and to continue to develop confidence at such a difficult time was important too. You should always play to your strengths, and fortunately for us we had an excellent choir, which most of the children seriously affected by Saffie's death belonged to. We didn't shy away from performing or from the songs we chose, as we were telling our story as part of our recovery. At an event we participated in at the Guild Hall in Preston, we sung 'Don't Look Back in Anger'. At this stage, everyone had stopped asking us how we were. Death is such a funny thing; people are afraid to put it on the table and discuss it, but the audience showed us they were with us. The huge hall was in darkness, with the exception of the spotlight brightly lighting up our choir, their distinctive navy-and-red tartan uniforms adding colour to the pale white of their faces. They started singing. You could tell they were nervous, but as they continued, they grew in confidence. I sat there with a governor and other staff, watching them. I could see from some of their faces that something was going on in the audience and, as I turned round to see, there was the most wonderful thing. Nearly everyone had taken out their phones and had switched their torches on. There were around two thousand people in the Grand Hall, lights moving in time to the music. It was such a beautiful sight, and I had a lump in my throat, while others in our party wiped away tears. Our children weren't forgotten, and that meant a lot to them and to the school. At the end of the performance some of the girls physically bounced off the stage. Any risks we had taken in our song choice had paid off. Moments like this certainly supported their recovery.

While there were always choices to be made, to do or not do something in the best interests of the children, there were external pressures where you would have to show strength of character and mind to justify your viewpoint. The Ofsted report was an achievement for the school, as we had not only dealt with the issues that had arisen due to the Manchester Arena attack, but had worked hard in all areas of framework to continuously improve. At this time, one of the big issues in education was around counterterrorism and the Prevent strategy. Up until May 2017, like most schools, we paid lip service to this, as I never thought we would be affected in this way. I hadn't put the paperwork in place, as I had so many priorities in my first year in the role. An issue that came about after the attack was the lockdown policy, which we had in place, but you were supposed to practice it regularly in case someone posing a risk obtained entry to the building. With other senior leaders in the school, we discussed it on many occasions, always coming to the same conclusion: we couldn't get the staff or children to practice it. It would have meant barricading themselves in rooms. Putting it that simply, it was obvious that we couldn't do this. I felt that it would be emotionally abusive to do so and, on the rare occasion I needed to debate it, the other person backed down – how could they not?

A sad reality is that we did need to consider elements of our curriculum, and also had to be careful about turns of phrases steeped in the English language that could easily cause offence to our children and be traumatic. Just imagine if a teacher had returned to a messy classroom from a course and said, 'What's happened here, children? It looks like a bomb's gone off.' For a couple of years I had purposely avoided holding assemblies on 5 November, when usually the children would be learning about Guy Fawkes and the infamous Gunpowder Plot of 1605. I had assumed that, as it was something steeped in our country's history, children would have had good knowledge of it anyway. I was wrong. When I did get back to leading an assembly on it, they were totally unaware. In fact, there was only one child who could tell me anything about it. The irony of that child being American did put a smile on my face, though. Moving forward, we will have to work on areas like this.

Our work on tolerance was vitally important, and we may never know the real impact that this has had. Although our approach was well received by parents and our community, it still saddened me that a minority could have such hatred, something that could easily be picked up by a child and taken into their adulthood for the whole cycle to start again. Strangely, when I first saw my job advertised in 2016, if you searched for information about Tarleton Community Primary School, images were brought up of anti-Islamic graffiti saying, 'No Muslims', on two of the large doors in our Early Years outdoor area. This had occurred in 2005, and there had been similar graffiti around the two villages of Tarleton and Hesketh Bank. Schools and head teachers are in a privileged position to be able to challenge such views, so that children are tolerant, leading to full and enriched lives. Education is a powerful and uniting tool. While people always bang on about the teaching of British values, here we were in the real world. This wasn't a tick box for an inspection, a comment on a website, or a nice display in the hall – the work we had done in transition with these pupils needed to be embedded into our curriculum.

I started researching, and one name kept coming up: Andrew Moffat. Andrew was a senior leader at Parkfield Community School in an area of Birmingham, not too far from Spaghetti Junction. He is a pioneer within the area of equalities education, quite rightly recognised through various awards, including an MBE, and had founded a charity called No Outsiders. The charity's approach covered all aspects of the protected characteristics within the Equality Act, but elements had not been popular with the majority Muslim community and parents at his school, specifically around the area of LGBT issues and the acknowledgement of same-sex relationships. This had hit the media, with protests outside of the school gates, and everything had become very unpleasant, causing the school to pause the programme while it worked with the DfE and its community to resolve any issues, which it eventually did.

This didn't put me off: in fact, quite the opposite. Why shouldn't children understand same-sex relationships? All families are different, and nobody should be respected less or treated any differently. My own openly gay sister had once had a disgusting comment directed towards her, from a very distant and religious family member. They had stated that they had to have a shower after being in her presence, because she was a lesbian. How ridiculous.

I wanted to go to Birmingham and meet Andrew. I stalked him on Twitter, messaging him, which paid off, as he invited me down to Parkfield. I invited other head teachers to join me, but they simply weren't interested, which was a shame. So I went with one of my governors, and one of my teachers who led in this area. We met early one morning for the long drive down the M6 to Birmingham. It was certainly a worthwhile trip. Andrew and his story blew us away, as did the No Outsiders approach. Our visit was symbolic to Andrew and some of the other teachers at the school, as the approach had only recently started up again from its pause and he didn't know what the feedback from children would be after when we visited various classes with different-aged children. In each class, the relationship he had with those children and staff was clear to see. He would ask them to tell us about No Outsiders, and they could. They would say that no one was the same and that everyone was different, identifying ways that they were different, including skin colour, hair colour, boys and girls. Everything, except that some people were gay and some were not. Secretly, all three of us hoped a child would say it, as we went into each room. Finally, in the last room, one little girl did. One of the teachers was in tears listening to her children talk about No Outsiders. It was obviously important to them, and the staff had been on such a rollercoaster journey of their own. Driving back from Birmingham, I thought about the day and the irony that No Outsiders had so offended members of the Islamic faith, while we wanted to use it in part to promote tolerance of all faiths, including Islam. What a funny world we live in. We are now proudly a No Outsiders school.

Colleagues in the area of mental health have always been interested not only in supporting us, but also in learning from us. I think this is because of the age of our children and how they were affected – it was such a unique situation. It would have been easy to turn down conversations or opportunities to work with those colleagues, but it wouldn't have been right. By sharing what we had experienced and what we had done effectively afterwards, others could learn and benefit. I think of all the faces of our children who suffered so badly, and of their parents. How could you not want to do your best to stop others from being affected in the future? I was approached by the Anna Freud Centre, a mental health charity, and met with them to discuss our learning. They were in the process of developing an initiative called the UK Trauma Council (UKTC). I had agreed to support them with a video case study to inform their work, something I was really interested in. Other professionals from a range of contexts and experiences were doing the same, for example, those involved with the Grenfell Tower disaster. Unfortunately, this plan was scuppered by the pandemic. It was, however, reassuring to know that school senior leadership teams were going to be better supported, In the pipeline was a portfolio of evidenced-based and accessible resources, so that leaders would have the tools to plan and immediately respond to critical incidents affecting schools more effectively. People were getting it. They were getting the mental health implications of all this, something which had been evident when I attended the National Emergencies Trust launch, but it didn't always feel like that. Organisations seemed to respond to the initial aftermath, then disappear. We must learn from everything that has happened and consider and put in place more medium- and long-term strategies, as terrorism doesn't just affect those present at the incident, or the families of those who sadly lost their lives or were injured, but instead ripples through society. A greater understanding of mental health support must be established, and there are lots of different angles to this.

One of the angles is around leadership during an incident. I worked with psychologists from Manchester University on a resource which focused on the responsibility and pressure on school leaders, and how they can fail to recognise pressures on themselves. I had had a couple of wobbles at certain points over the last few years, but had recognised this and managed to keep going. Supervision certainly supported me with this and, in finding it and developing systems for my staff, it may well have made that difference. I was pleased to be involved in the project with Manchester University.

The journey of leading our school through recovery had been a long and winding path, at times devastating and at times remarkable. The question from one of our mothers, about when the sparkle in her little girl's eyes would come back, was really what it was about for all of our children: *how do we do this?* Keeping things simple is what it was all about. That is where thinking differently, finding the positives where there are few, has to happen. Day after day we painted smiles on our faces and got on with it. Some days we won, others we lost; but, as a school, we kept going. There was no other choice. We all learned and shared so much. We battled, at times, against systems that needed updating and against those who snubbed us in our attempts to affect change, thinking that we would go away. This is why we are so proud of our work with the DfE, and of seeing the work of the National Emergencies Trust and the UK Trauma Council come to fruition. Others, like us, had seen the gap, and although this couldn't now benefit us, it could help so many in the future. There are good people out there, and to do nothing in circumstances such as these would be a crime in itself.

My final words must go to a little girl whom we all miss terribly, and to her incredibly brave family. The Roussos family were just a normal family, and we should all pause for a moment to think about their experiences through all of this. This will be the same for all of the families of the twenty-two victims. Someone you love with all your heart is there, having one of the best evenings of their lives, and then they are taken from you, in such a senseless and cowardly act. That empty void, those angry questions, are endless. As time goes on, when you find the answers, they become more and more impossible to internalise.

Saffie was a free spirit, and so we must remember her that way. She died, but she also lived a short but very happy life, surrounded by love and friendship. She entertained, she laughed, she danced, and she did all the things that a little girl should. I am proud to have known this wonderful little girl, whose outlook on life was and still is an inspiration to us all. So, as you close this book today and go about your business, try to be more like

Saffie: ambitious, good-humoured, loving, and compassionate. The world will truly be a better place.

Sleep tight, superstar.

Printed in Great Britain
by Amazon